CHARLES PEIRCE'S PRAGMATIC PLURALISM

SUNY Series in Philosophy
George R. Lucas, Jr., Editor

CHARLES PEIRCE'S PRAGMATIC PLURALISM

SANDRA B. ROSENTHAL

Loyola University, New Orleans

State University
of New York
Press

I would like to thank the editors of the following journals for permission to republish all or parts of the following articles: *Transactions of the Charles S. Peirce Society: A Quarterly Journal in American Philosopihy:* "The Pragmatic World of Charles Peirce," XIX (1983), "Peirce's Ultimate Logical Interpretant and the Dynamical Object: A Pragmatic Perspective," XXVI (1990), "Temporality, Perceptual Experience, and Peirce's Proofs of Realism," XX, 1984; *The Monist:* "Meaning as Habit: Some Systematic Implications of Peirce's Pragmatism," 65 (1982); *International Philosophical Quarterly:* "Mathematical Necessity, Scientific Fallibilism, and Pragmatic Verificationalism: The Peircean Synthesis," XXIV, 1984; *The Journal of the History of Philosophy,* "Peirce's Theory of the Perceptual Judgment" 7 (1969).
Published by
State University of New York Press, Albany

Production by Susan Geraghty
Marketing by Nancy Farrell

Printed in the United States of America

For information, address State University of New York
Press, State University Plaza, Albany, N.Y., 12246

Library of Congress Cataloging-in-Publication Data

Rosenthal, Sandra B.
Charles Peirce's pragmatic pluralism / Sandra B. Rosenthal.
p. cm. — (SUNY series in philosophy)
Includes bibliographical references and index.
ISBN 0-7914-2157-0 (alk. paper). — ISBN 0-7914-2158-9 (pbk. : alk. paper)
1. Peirce, Charles S. (Charles Sanders), 1839–1914.
2. Pragmatism—History—19th century. 3. Pluralism—History—19th century. I. Title. II. Series.
B945.P44R68 1994
191—dc20 93-46977
CIP

10 9 8 7 6 5 4 3 2 1

For Rogene
My own little miracle

CONTENTS

INTRODUCTION

In recent Peirce scholarship, in the form of books, articles, and papers, one finds growing flirtations, albeit tentative and brief, with pluralistic dimensions of Peirce's thought, largely brought about by, and explicitly linked with, the Kuhnsian interpretation of the scientific enterprise. Piecemeal pluralism, however, does not work, and if the search for pluralism in Peirce's thought remains unsystematic, then tentativeness is indeed required, for such a search eventually stumbles on the seeming bedrock of his position: his claims of the convergence toward the final ultimate opinion of the community of interpreters in the idealized long run. This work is an attempt to jump off the deep end, so to speak, and elicit the inherent strand of pragmatic pluralism that is embedded in the very core of Peirce's thought and that weaves his various doctrines into a systematic pattern of pluralism that gives a new design to his understanding of convergence.

The bedrock of convergence seemingly becomes even more formidable when given the added strength of Peirce's emphatic and often quoted statement made in a letter to William James that "pluralism does not satisfy either my head or my heart."[1] Yet, when this statement is contextually located, its complexion changes, for as he continues, "I am as sure as I am of anything that the logical doctrines connected with it,—Achilles and the Tortoise, etc.,—are utterly false."[2] This reference to the well-known paradox makes clear that Peirce is here hitting the pluralism of nominalism with its discrete units, a view that he counters with his emphasis on continuity or synechism. And it is this emphasis on continuity or synechism that provides a major fiber in the systematic pattern of his own unique pluralism, a pluralism that attacks the "pluralism of nominalism" and its related logical doctrines with the vengeance he desires, but which cannot be articulated piecemeal. The present endeavor will incorporate a number of my own previous articles on Peirce's philosophy that, because they are themselves "piecemeal," fail to recognize the radical pluralism implicit in the interpretations of Peirce's philosophy that they present.

The question of the scope of pragmatism in general and of Peirce's pragmatism in particular has been a lively topic of debate for years.[3] This work takes the scope and significance of Peirce's pragmatism in a broad sense that many will dispute. It holds that his pragmatism cannot be contained within the narrow confines frequently allotted it. Rather it overflows such limited boundaries, embedding within numerous philosophic areas and issues pragmatic characteristics that elude traditional labels and traditional alternatives. The following pages are in a sense an attempt to justify a broad reading of the nature, scope, and significance of Peirce's pragmatism that, again, is suggested in necessarily piecemeal, inadequate fashion in some of my previous articles.

There are some claims made in the following pages that, to my mind, virtually call out for comparison with similar doctrines touched upon by other pragmatists, and many of my previous works have focused on the mutual clarification of Peirce and one or several of the other classical American pragmatists concerning various issues discussed throughout the following pages. The deliberate omission of references to other pragmatists in this work is intended to support the present interpretation of Peirce's philosophy in the sense of showing that the deeply rooted and pervasive, pragmatically oriented pluralism that this study attempts to elicit can "stand on its own two feet" in light of Peirce's own writings.

Finally, the objection may be raised that there is an obvious selectivity running through the present focus on Peirce's writings. This cannot be denied. Given the nature of the corpus of Peirce's writings, however, selectivity must be evinced in any attempt to highlight dimensions of a consistent position. What makes selectivity particularly noticeable in the following pages is that the passages selected are at times not the passages typically, if ever, chosen to be quoted in Peirce scholarship. Various lights can be cast on Peirce's position by approaching it from various perspectives. Other perspectives may be equally or more fruitful for specific purposes. The purpose of this work is to cast a novel light upon Peirce's thinking in a way that can perhaps prove fruitful for reassessing his relevance for some key contemporary issues.

The first chapter will elicit pluralistic dimensions in Peirce's understanding of world, truth, and science that place his philosophy of science squarely in the camp of the Kuhnsian position. From the backdrop of this affinity, the following chapters will detail the pluralism inherent in key facets of Peirce's thought. This will show that running through the very core of his philosophy is a pluralism that provides the needed epistemic, and correlative metaphysical, underpinnings for a solid philosophical grounding of the Kuhnsian interpretation of science. At the same time, it will both reveal a systematic unity to Peirce's work and offer resolutions for some of the problems, tensions, and inconsistencies often attributed to his position.

Chapter 2 examines Peirce's understanding of meaning as habit from the backdrop of his mathematical writings. This exploration attempts to show that his understanding of the certitude and specificity of mathematical truths involves an analytic-synthetic distinction that points toward an implicit yet pervasive and significant functioning of an analytic-synthetic distinction in his understanding of empirical knowledge. The functioning of this distinction is uniquely pragmatic in tone, and it lays the foundation for a strain of radical pluralism that permeates his philosophy and sheds light on his pluralistic understanding of both the relation between the ultimate logical interpretant and the dynamical object and what is "given" in the sensing dimension of experience.

Chapter 3 attempts to clarify and interrelate Peirce's proofs for realism, showing that the contradictions that they supposedly contain can be integrated into a unified view in a way that helps lay the foundation for a pluralistic reading of his position.

The following chapter focuses on Peirce's experimental derivation of the categories and the pluralism that is built into this very method of eliciting them. This experimental method, with its pluralistic implications, not only holds for the derivation of both his phenomenological and metaphysical categories but also characterizes the nature of the relation between them.

In Chapter 5, the content of Peirce's metaphysics is explored. This examination shows the distinctively pragmatic flavor of his metaphysical claims and indicates as well that his understanding of the nature of reality is not of a type that could provide the basis for an ideally true and final opinion or support the drive toward unanimity in final knowledge. Rather, his understanding of reality provides the needed metaphysical underpinnings for a Kuhnsian-Peircean interpretation of science as presented in the first chapter.

CHAPTER 1

World, Truth, and Science

Peirce's position is usually held to lie in radical opposition to the Kuhnsian interpretation of science. Depending upon one's opinion of Kuhn's views, this opposition has been seen as contributing to the strength of Peirce's position or as rendering it outdated. And, while some recent Peirce literature has pointed out flirtatious moments of reconciliatory pluralism in Peirce's position, such claims are brief and halting, tend to touch only the periphery of Peirce's thought, and are in the minority by far. This chapter proposes to lay out an interpretation of Peirce's philosophy of science that is inherently pluralistic, shows the philosophic kinship of Peirce and Kuhn, and points toward a solid philosophical grounding of the Kuhnsian interpretation of science.

The lack of such a philosophical grounding is in fact the basis for the by now well-plowed field of criticisms hurled at Kuhn's *Structure of Scientific Revolutions.* His denial of the empiricist dogma that there is a permanent neutral observation language, that there must be a neutral epistemological framework to evaluate competing theories and paradigms, or that there is a discoverable set of rules for the resolution of conflicting statements, combined with his notion of persuasion and his radical claim that at the most fundamental level of incommensurability scientists are practicing in different worlds and seeing different things, has led to charges of subjectivism, relativism, irrationalism, and the denial of scientific progress. Kuhn's own recognition of the dilemma of rejecting long held foundationalist interpretations of scientific method while having no adequate philosophical alternative to replace them is well evinced in his own words:

> But is sensory experience fixed and neutral? Are theories simply man-made interpretations of given data? The epistemological viewpoint that has most often guided Western philosophy for three centuries dictates an immediate and unequivocal Yes! *In the absence of a developed alternative,* I find it impossible to relin-

> quish entirely that viewpoint. Yet it no longer functions effectively, and the attempts to make it do so through the introduction of a neutral language of observations now seem to me hopeless.[1]

It is precisely such a "developed alternative," which undercuts the objectivism-relativism, foundationalism-antifoundationalism issue, that will be provided by the present interpretation of Peirce's position. And, since Kuhn holds that at the most fundamental level of incommensurability scientists are practicing in different worlds and seeing different things, it is with Peirce's concept of 'world' that the ensuing endeavor can best begin.

Peirce never explicitly clarifies his understanding of "the real world," though he refers to it frequently throughout his writings. Such a lack of explicit clarification can well go unremarked, for it is a commonsense term that slides easily—indeed too easily—into a commonsense identification with "what is the case" or "what there is." The ultimate nature of "what there is" may receive various philosophic labels, depending upon whether one interprets Peirce as a realist, an idealist, or a phenomenalist, but the unquestioned commonsense identification of "what there is" with Peirce's statements concerning the real world is the unquestioned basis for the application of these labels in many instances. When such an identification is questioned, however, and Peirce's various statements concerning the real world are interrelated for a development of their systematic import, it will be seen that "the real world" fits inadequately within the confines of any of the above labels, for it is a distinctively pragmatic world.

The following discussion proposes to show that Peirce, in rejecting the role of humans as spectators, in understanding experience as a unity of interaction between humans and that facticity that gives itself within experience, can hold at once that the real world is the perceived world,[2] that the real world has an independence from mind,[3] and yet that the perceived world is partially dependent upon the noetic act and is thus relative in its nature to the mind.[4] The supposed incompatibility of these three characteristics of the relation of thought to the real world stems from failure to radically and once and for all reject the presuppositions of a spectator theory of knowledge.[5] Peirce's absolute and radical rejection of the spectator theory of knowledge gives rise to, and is in turn brought into clearer light by, an understanding of his pragmatic concept of 'world'.

That the real world is the perceived world is clearly indicated by Peirce in several succinct passages. He states that "The real world is the world of sensible experience;"[6] or, in other terms, the real world is the world of "insistent generalized percepts,"[7] which are not representative of any underlying reality other than themselves.[8] The real world can be characterized, also, as the world of perceptual facts, for "what I carry with me" of the percept "is the perceptual facts."[9] Such a world is a consistent system of facts rigorously obeying the laws of non-contradiction and excluded middle, for "Dichotomy rules the ideal world,"[10] and "it is part of the process of sensible experience to locate its facts in the world of ideas."[11] Such a grasping of the sensible world in terms of a system of ideas is of the very essence of the sensible world. As Peirce stresses, "This is what I mean by saying that the sensible world is but a fragment of the ideal world."[12]

Further, the system of ideas or meanings in some sense limits the facts which may occur "in the world," for "We know in advance of experience that certain things are not true, because we see they are impossible. . . . I know it is not true, because I satisfy myself that there is no room for it even in that ideal world of which the real world is but a fragment."[13] Thus, what can occur "in the world" must conform to the possibilities allowed for by the world of ideas or the system of meanings in terms of which we approach it. To better understand what can possibly occur in the world, it will be helpful at this point to turn to a closer examination of the various senses of "possible" in Peirce's philosophy as they relate to the issue of world.

When Peirce speaks of "possible experience," he at times means possible in the sense of "consistently thinkable" and at times in the nonepistemically related sense of metaphysically possible.[14] However, "possible" in the sense of consistently thinkable is open to some misunderstanding if not further clarified. In addition to making the distinction between the consistently thinkable and the metaphysically possible, Peirce distinguishes between what he calls the "essentially" or "logically" possible and the "substantially" possible.[15] This latter distinction cannot be equated with the former but can best be understood as a distinction within the consistently thinkable. Essential possibility means, for Peirce, logical conceivability or the absence of self-contradiction. Substantial possibility, however, refers to the relation that something considered has to information of the present in the present. In this sense possible means consistent with everything known about the real world. Possible in this second sense seems to indicate a type of "physical possibility." And, while substantial possibility must imply essential possibility, essential possibility need not imply substantial possibility, for of those possible combinations that "occur in the ideal world, some do and some do not occur in the real world; but all that occur in the real world occur also in the ideal world."[16]

Here, however, it must be noted that if a proposition that is essentially possible but not substantially possible is combined with the body of given information, a logically or essentially impossible set results, for "Two propositions contradictory of one another may both be severally possible, although their combination is not possible."[17] As Peirce further observes, "It is an anacoluthon to say that a proposition is impossible because it is self-contradictory. It rather is thought so as to appear self-contradictory because the ideal induction has shown it to be impossible."[18] Thus, at any time, a range of what is substantially possible may be determined ideally or logically, though what specific possibility will in fact be actualized in the future cannot be determined in this manner, for there are, indeed, "future contingents."[19]

This point, however, leads directly away from the above issue of the human way of knowing to the related issue of reality's way of being, for to conclude from the above discussion "that there is nothing analogous to possibility" in reality, but that this mode appertains "only to the particular limited information we possess, would be even less defensible than to draw precisely the opposite conclusion from the same premisses. It is a style of reasoning most absurd."[20] Though substantive possibility, which in its broadest sense determines what may occur "in the world," cannot be understood apart from the knowledge structure that grasps, this does not lead to a conventionalism, for the real world is a special "part of the ideal world. Namely, that part which sufficient experience would tend ultimately (and therefore definitively) to compel Reason to acknowledge as having a being independent of what he may arbitrarily, or willfully, create."[21] To further understand the nature of the world as a consistent system of facts, then, it will be necessary to turn to an examination of the independently real and the metaphysical sense of the possibilities within the real world.

It has been seen that dichotomy rules the real world, because it rules the ideal world of which the real world is a part. Yet Peirce's view of the nature of the real as independent of the human mode of grasping it indicates that such hard discrete exactitudes do not exist, for reality, according to Peirce, is a continuum that "swims in indeterminacy."[22] For this reason, the principle of continuity, which pervades the independently real, is "fallibilism objectified."[23] Further, the independently real as a continuum of events is precisely that to which neither the law of noncontradiction nor the law of excluded middle is perfectly applicable.[24]

Thus, it would seem that though the hereness and nowness of events and the continuities that pervade them are independent of our conceptualizations and the possibilities that they allow, what the hereness and nowness can consistently be held to be is partially determined by the range of conceptual or ideal possibilities within which discrete facts can consistently emerge. As Peirce observes, what is demanded "above all is the fact and the admission that the world is reasonable—reasonably susceptible to becoming reasonable, for that is what it is, and all that it is, to be reasonable."[25] From this perspective, it can perhaps be said that what *occurs* must be metaphysically possible, while *what* occurs must be epistemically or conceptually possible as well.[26]

The relation between the continuum of qualitative events that constitutes the character of the metaphysically real independently of the human mode of grasping, and the system of facts that constitutes the real world, is brought into focus by Peirce's discussion of the relation between events or occurrences and facts:

> I must first point out the distinction between a Fact and what in other connexions, is often called an Event but which, owing to that word being used in the Doctrines of Chances in its stricter sense . . . must be here called an Occurrence. An Occurrence, which Thought analyzes into Things and Happenings, is necessarily Real; but it can never be known or even imagined in all its infinite detail. A Fact, on the other hand is so much of the real Universe as can be represented in a Proposition, and instead of being, like an Occurrence, a slice of the Universe, it is rather to be

> compared to a chemical principle extracted therefrom by the power of Thought; and though it is, or may be Real, yet, in its Real existence it is inseparably combined with an infinite swarm of circumstances, which make no part of the Fact itself. It is impossible to thread our way through the Logical intricacies of being unless we keep these two things, the Occurrence and the Real Fact, sharply separate in our Thoughts.[27]

Here lies the significance of Peirce's claim that "Nature, in connection with a picture, copy, or diagram does not necessarily denote an object not fashioned by man, but merely the object represented as something existing apart from the representation."[28] Mill's failure to recognize this mind relatedness of worldly nature, according to Peirce, led him astray in his analysis of the "uniformity of nature."[29]

Peirce indicates the above position from a slightly different direction in his cryptic claim that "The inkstand is a real thing. Of course in being real and external, it does not in the least cease to be a purely psychical product, a generalized percept."[30] Or as he elaborates, a "this" is an object selected by a subject from the continuum of possibility.[31] Reality independent of our thinking exerts an influence on our ways of thinking about it, but what facts and objects it contains is partially dependent upon the conceptual framework in terms of which we delineate objects and facts within the backdrop of a world. Indeed, according to Peirce "External Fact" can change in accordance with the way human minds "feel, think, or suffer."[32] Peirce offers a helpful clarification about his limited intentions in his numerous statements concerning the independence of real objects, claiming that, the real object can be "an object shaped by thinking. . . ; but so far as it is Real, it is not modified by thinking *about it*."[33] Such an interactional context is highlighted in John Lachs' claim that for Peirce, "We thus find the world, partly at least, a social product and ourselves the divine comakers of reality."[34]

The failure to distinguish between the metaphysical possibilities contained in and giving rise to emerging occurrences and the logical or epistemic possibilities that allow us to grasp occurrences in such a way as to give rise to a consistent system of facts results in the identification of ontological possibility with some type of Platonic essence.[35] The possibility of the ideal world, of which the sensible world is but a fragment, is not another Platonic world that in some way allows the actual sensible world to participate in reality but is an ideal world of logical possibilities whose structure is dependent upon human intelligence: "It has come about through the agencies of development that man is endowed with intelligence of such a nature that he can by ideal experiments ascertain that in a certain universe of logical possibility certain combinations occur while others do not."[36] Thus, it is through developing human intelligence that there is an "evolution of Platonic Forms."[37] Evolving concepts are analogous to "Platonic Forms," not in the sense of being metaphysical essences, but in the sense that each successive concept can itself be characterized as fixed, eternal, unchanging, and, indeed, "toward the side of math."[38] For, according to Peirce, meanings do not literally change; instead, a new meaning replaces an old meaning. Though the same words may be used, there is a substitution of the meanings or concepts attached to them.[39] Thus Peirce, in the context of discussing the semiotic interrelationship of ground, object, and interpretant, can hold that ideas are "to be understood in a sort of Platonic sense."[40]

In short, the ideal world as indicating a realm of logical possibilities within which the actual world must be located is not some realm of metaphysical forms; indeed, it is not a topic for metaphysics at all but rather belongs to the area of epistemology. The ideal world is the conceptual world of the logically possible or the consistently thinkable within which the facts of experience must be located. To turn the conceptual realm into the metaphysical realm is a reification that obscures the character of the independently real, the character of our mode of grasping the independently real, and the character of the world as that which emerges through their interaction. From this backdrop, the following discussion can now turn to a general characterization of such an emerging world.

The above analysis has attempted to show that the real world is ontologically one with independent reality as an infinitely rich continuum of qualitative events. It is, metaphysically, that independently real. Yet a world is dependent upon the meaning system that grasps in a way in which reality as independent is not, for a world is that perspective of the infinitely rich reality that has been "fixed" or "carved out" by a system of ideas. Knowledge is abstractive and selective. A world, though concrete, is nonetheless selective in the sense that a world, as the concrete content denoted by a system of meanings, is a way in which the concreteness of reality can be delineated or "fixed." A system, once chosen, limits the alternatives possible within it, but alternative systems may be possible. As Peirce notes, "Truly natural classes may, and undoubtedly often do, merge into one another inextricably,"[41] and thus boundary lines must be imposed, although the classes are natural.[42] The continuity is there; where the "cut" is imposed is, in part, our decision. Like the boundary lines of natural classes, the "boundary lines" that constitute the world may have been differently drawn, giving rise to different possibilities within the world. A world is delineated by a system of facts, but facts are not independent of the selective knowledge process, for facts are abstracted portions of a continuum of events.

A world is by definition consistent because a world is the concrete content that is delineated by a set of consistent propositions. The world answers to the laws of excluded middle and noncontradiction, and thus it represents the ideal of that which has been conceptually articulated—and hence made precise—to its ideal limit. "The world," then, is at once the basis for every experience and the ideal of a complete synthesis of possible experience. Perhaps it can be said, somewhat metaphorically, that while reality is the infinity of a continuum or ongoing process, the world is the logical fixation of an infinite number of possible cuts within it. Thus, the world is the context of meaning within which all other frameworks and objects may be articulated, in the sense that the world is the "outermost" content or encompassing frame of reference of the application of a set of meaning structures to the independently real and hence of the propositions that can delineate experience consistently within the context of these meanings. Such a world, then, opens in one direction toward the structures of the independently real and the possibilities it presents and in the other direction toward the structures of our modes of grasping the independently real and the possibilities such modes of grasping allow. What can occur in the world must conform to the possibilities available within the world we have structured—though the world we have structured has arisen through the successful interaction with the possibilities offered by the independently real. Peirce's concept of world has significant implications for issues of truth and science. The following pages will focus on each of these issues both in turn and in their interrelation.

The extent of the radical conflict of interpretations concerning

Peirce's theory of truth in the literature is perhaps best captured in Robert Almeder's claim that the literature on Peirce contains "no fewer than thirteen distinct interpretations of Peirce's views on the nature of truth."[43] Within Peirce scholarship, the acceptance of convergence and the final ultimate opinion transcends the realist-idealist controversy, though the understanding of the nature of the final ultimate opinion as that toward which inquiry on any subject will converge will vary according to camps. Thus, a realist interpretation holds that "The opinion reached in the final opinion, unlike opinions reached earlier, shall never be overthrown although the degree to which the final opinion *corresponds* to fact admits of indefinite, (but not substantial) refinement."[44] While, as has been stated from the backdrop of a coherence theory of truth, the true bedrock of pragmatism is "ultimately the entire framework of objective logic and objective idealism."[45]

Before examining Peirce's theory of truth in relation to traditional alternatives of correspondence or coherence, it will be helpful to clarify at this point the type of realism involved in discussing the correspondence theory of truth, for it is not the realism that lies in opposition to nominalism and asserts the reality of universals. Nor is the point at issue the question of the externality of the real; rather, it is the relation of the externally real to the knower. What the present rejection of the label of "realism" does and does not imply can best be brought to light by way of comparison with Almeder's espousal of Peirce's "epistemological realism." He proceeds by showing that Peirce is not a phenomenalist and not an idealist and that Peirce offers a defense of belief in the existence of an external reality, a reality, moreover, with which the knower is in direct contact.[46] With these points the present interpretation agrees. But what this realism also includes for Almeder, as well as for most who accept the realist label, is that the sense in which the real external world we know "is dependent on mind turns out to be *trivially* true and necessary for any epistemological realism wherein it is a necessary condition that the external world be knowable."[47] Or as such a realism is elsewhere characterized, "There is a *world of objects* whose properties are neither logically nor causally dependent upon the noetic act of any number of finite minds."[48]

It is these generally held assumptions associated with the realist label that are denied in denying that Peirce is a realist, for, as seen above, the world and the objects within it are partially dependent upon the noetic acts of finite minds. Thus, while Peirce cannot be called an "idealist"[49] or a "phenomenalist," neither can he be called a "realist." For, though Peirce holds we are in direct contact with an external "brutely there" reality that limits our interpretations, thus rendering the coherence theory of truth incomplete, the relation of the knower to this known external reality cannot be understood in terms of correspondence. And, although it may well be an oversimplification to say that coherence theories of truth belong to idealism while correspondence theories of truth belong to realism, an interpretation of Peirce as an epistemological realist in the above sense indicated by Almeder and accepted by most others using this label leads to the view that at least the ideally true and final opinion on any matter would involve a relation of correspondence.[50] To the question, what alternative remains when one rules out the correspondence of realism as well as the coherence of idealism,[51] the answer is, the pragmatic alternative. Peirce's pragmatic theory of truth is ultimately intertwined not just with his understanding of scientific method as the method of fixing belief but also with the entire gamut of his unique pragmatic epistemology and metaphysics.[52]

Because for Peirce the hereness and nowness of events and the real connections they display is independent of, yet enters directly into interaction with, our conceptualizations and the possibilities they allow, coherence or consistency is not a sufficient criterion for the truth of empirical assertions. There must be a pragmatic interplay between our concepts and actual experience. There is an ontological dimension to what appears within experience that limits our interpretations in terms of workability. But true knowledge, even ideally true knowledge, could not be correspondence, for the nature of our intentional link with reality through conceptual structures, and the nature of reality as a continuum that "swims" in indeterminacy, makes the relation of correspondence literally senseless. Rather, Peirce claims that a true thought is one that *answers*, that leads to thoughts in harmony with nature.[53] The relation of "answering" is ultimately two directional. Reality answers our questions and determines the workability of our meaning structures, but what answers it gives are partially dependent on what questions we ask, and what meaning structures work are partially dependent upon the structures we bring. Truth is always worldly truth, for "nothing else than a Fact possibly can be a 'witness' or 'testimony,'"[54] and facts, it will be remembered, are always relative to the framework of a discriminating mind. Yet the witness of a fact is the real, "since it is truly in that which occurs."[55]

Worldly truth is thus perspectival, and other perspectives are always possible. Truth involves convergence, but convergence within a common world that we have partially made and continually remake in various of its aspects. Thus Peirce, in speaking of truth, whether "scientific, moral, metaphysical, or common sense,"[56] states that "the perfect truth of a statement requires that it should involve the confession that the perfect doctrine can neither be stated nor conceived."[57] Again, Peirce claims that an essential ingredient of truth includes a confession of its "one-sidedness."[58] That this is intended not as a factual limitation on present knowledge but as a theoretical limitation due to the nature of knowledge is found in Peirce's comparison of the ideal limit of convergence, the ideal of a "final ultimate opinion," to the ideal limit of pi. It is "an ideal limit to which no numerical expression can be perfectly true."[59] It is an unattainable ideal not only in fact but also by the very nature of that which sets the ideal limit.[60] Thus Peirce can present the following hypothetical situation:

> Suppose our opinion with reference to a given question to be quite settled, so that inquiry, no matter how far pushed, has no surprises for us on this point. Then we may be said to have attained *perfect knowledge* about that question. True, it is conceivable that somebody else would attain to a like perfect knowledge which should conflict with ours. This is conceivable.[61]

Peirce then goes on to say that though it is theoretically possible it is not practically possible "considering the social nature of man," for we would "compare notes; and if we never do compare notes, and no third party talks with both and makes the comparison, it is difficult to see what meaning there is in saying we disagree."[62] That Peirce is not using the term "perfect knowledge" in a loose commonsense way can be seen from his explicit distinction between it and "practically perfect belief."[63] Thus even the ideal of convergence to a final ultimate opinion, to perfect knowledge, is always convergence within an accepted framework or perspective. And there are always other and possibly better ways of cutting into reality, of delineating the context within which convergence can occur. This is implied by the very nature of reality as a continuum that swims in indeterminacy. Thus convergence toward one final truth is "a regulative principle, an intellectual hope," and such a rule of hope must be followed, for "despair is insanity."[64] Yet even such a rule of hope, the "cheerful hope" that animates the followers of science, involves "*something approximating*" only,[65] for the "indeterminate" nature of reality may mean that concerning "*the* answer, that is, the final answer . . . there is none."[66] H. S. Thayer's characterization of Peirce's concept of truth as having the function of Kant's regulative ideas "serving as a working standard of criticism" would apply here, but at a more radical level than that intended by his characterization.[67]

The objects within our world do not copy the independently real but emerge through our modes of grasping the independently real. Nor do the modes of grasping via which emerge the objectivities within our world copy the independently real but rather they serve as conceptual tools for "cutting the edges" of the independently real continuum of events that "swims" in indeterminacy. The ideally true opinion would be that opinion that would perfectly work in anticipating possibilities of experience and would work, not because it adequately copied, but because it adequately "cut into" the independently real. Finally, the world within which specific meanings and beliefs arise, and within which objects or facts emerge for conscious awareness, is not a copy of an independent reality, nor is it identical with an independent reality in its character as independent. Rather, such a world is the encompassing frame of reference or field of interest of organism-environment interaction, the ultimate backdrop of rationality within which emerging facts are situated. And thus Peirce can proclaim that "In its proper meaning realism is a kind of idealism. It is the doctrine that ideas play a part in the real world."[68] This realism that is an idealism is in fact neither but is a manifestation of that thread of pragmatic pluralism that runs through his position, for this "realism [that] is a kind of idealism" emerges from his understanding of the pragmatic interplay between the indeterminately rich reality that offers its independent influence and the meanings by which we render it intelligible and suitable for our needs.

From the above pluralistic perspective, the concluding focus will turn to some issues in Peirce's philosophy of science. The literature on Peirce usually evinces the unquestioned assumption that he is a scientific realist. Thus, for example, Helmut Pape questions whether Peirce's conception of physical processes is consistent with his realistic interpretation of scientific concepts and theories,[69] while Robert Almeder claims that Peirce's position, in providing for the ontologically privileged position of science, runs counter to the relativity implicit in the commonly held view that there will always be competing alternative scientific theories.[70] Similarly, Bruce Altushuler claims that "the scientistic spirit of Peirce's perspective" would "make his analysis less than attractive to many these days."[71]

Yet, in recent literature on Peirce, this acceptance of his "scientific realism" is combined with flirtations with pluralism. Peter Skagestad can serve as a good example here, as can be seen from the following exchange. Focusing on a passage from Peirce in which he stresses "How much more the word *electricity* means now than it did in the days of Franklin; how much more the term planet means now than it did in the time (of) Hipparchus,"[72] Hjalmar Wennerberg objects that Peirce's theory "blurs the important distinction between logical analysis and empirical research."[73] To this view Skagestad responds that Peirce "does not blur this distinction in the least; he unconditionally denies that there is any such distinction."[74] He notes that Wennerberg's book was written before the appearance of Thomas Kuhn's *Structures of Scientific Revolutions*, thus resulting in his finding Peirce's position deficient because it does not hold to the distinction sufficiently clearly, while "Today, few thinkers familiar with the history of science would deny that scientific terms change their meanings through changes in scientific theory."[75]

What brings Peirce's position closer to Kuhn's ideas than even Skagestad allows, however, is precisely that Peirce neither ignores nor blurs the distinction but insists on upholding it, albeit implicitly so. What is operative in the process of meaning changes stressed above by Skagestad is precisely the distinction between the genetic origin of a system of concepts and the logical analysis of what they prescribe. If that which a meaning generates, or in other terms, contains, is too frequently inapplicable, our meanings may alter through the formation of new habits that creatively fixate inductively accumulated experiences in new ways. However, what we then have is a new meaning, or a new rule of generation of conditions of verification, which now necessarily contains at least partially different schematic possibilities.[76] It was seen above that Peirce holds that though the same words may be used, the meanings attached to them are different.[77] And thus he further claims that through a change of some part of a network of meanings, though not necessarily of words, what is inconceivable today may become conceivable tomorrow.[78]

Further, for Peirce, we test beliefs, not in isolation, but as parts of a whole set of claims.[79] Peirce holds that discrepancies between theory and observation can be interpreted either as observational errors[80] or as indicative of the need to alter the theory.[81] We should anticipate that data will arise that do not fit the theory[82] and hence that the above contextual decisions must be made. Something similar to auxiliary hypotheses in science is operative even in our commonsense awareness of the world around us. No part of a relevant corpus of knowledge is immune from change in the face of repeated disconfirming instances. Further, any part of a belief structure can be held in the face of disconfirming evidence by changing other parts of the structure.[83] Experience reveals that an improvement is necessary, but it does not specify which improvement is needed. Whether we change empirical generalizations in the face of disconfirming facts or restructure a set of meanings to allow the emergence of new facts is not itself dictated by the evidence, but is a pragmatic "decision" operative within the context of the encompassing intentional unity of humans and their world. And, indeed, experience usually proceeds without any awareness as to whether or not we have modified an empirical generalization by counterinstances, or have replaced a meaning to avoid having to "throw out" too much of experience as not real contents of a particular type, for such "pragmatic decisions" are implicit in modes of response.

The interconnected meanings of conceptual structure thus dictate what can conceivably be found in empirical research, while empirical research can lead to the overthrow of a system of logically interconnected meanings. Scientific revolutions are radical examples of the emergence of new conceptual structures, new meanings that legislate what facts conceivably may be or what facts are perceived. The recognition of such radical overthrows of conceptual frameworks is evinced in Peirce's emphasis on "Cataclysmal evolution,"[84] which, as opposed to both Darwinian and Lamarckian evolution, highlights the occurrence of breaks that are nonetheless not haphazard.[85] Peirce holds that such evolution is the chief factor not only in the evolution of living forms but also in the evolution of institutions and ideas.[86] As Peirce stresses, science advances mainly by cataclysmal evolution.[87] "It advances by leaps; and the impulse for each leap is either some new observational resource, or some novel way of reasoning. . . ." Moreover, a novel way of reasoning can itself be considered "a new observational means."[88]

The meaning structures of science change more rapidly and are more in conflict than the vague indubitables of common sense, though the dynamics operative in each level are the same. Common sense indubitables are "indubitable at the time being," and the changes are so slow that they can ordinarily be ignored.[89] Though the hypostatic abstractions or creative abductions that give rise to commonsense objects change so slowly that they can ordinarily be ignored, they are subject to alternatives nonetheless. Peirce gives examples from common sense and science to show that subjects are operations or qualities that have been transformed by hypostatic abstraction[90] and that hypostatic abstractions can be made in various ways, giving rise to different objects.[91]

Further, the world of science, far from being the ontologically privileged world, is dependent on the everyday world of common sense within which experience opens onto the indefinite richness of the ontologically real. The world of science is a second-level abstraction rooted in the world of common sense and opening onto the acritically indubitable but invariably vague beliefs of common sense. Peirce holds that the hypostatic abstractions of science are ultimately founded in the hypostatic abstractions that constitute percepts and, in fact, depend upon them for the very possibility of science. For "All science, without being aware of it, virtually supposes the truth of the vague results of uncontrolled thought upon such [commonsense] experience, cannot help doing so, and would have to shut up shop if she should manage to escape accepting them.[92] Scientific theories, rooted in everyday experience, are more imaginative, more of the nature of ideas,[93] and more precise than the commonsense experience that founds them. As such, they are more dubitable than the beliefs of common sense, for "the acritically indubitable is invariably vague."[94] As he emphasizes, it is "easy to be certain. One has only to be sufficiently vague."[95]

That there can be incommensurable scientific worlds that nonetheless have a shared meaningfulness rooted in the commonality of the relatively "acritically indubitable" but "invariably vague" commonsense world[96] is indicated in Peirce's claim that all humans have "some notion, however crude and concrete, of force, matter, space, and time," as well as some notion of "what sort of objects their fellow beings are," while "Modern science . . . has put us into quite another world; almost as much so as if it had transported our race to another planet."[97] Any scientific world opens onto the commonsense world that provides our concrete access to the indeterminate richness of the reality within which we are embedded, and thus "The instinctive result of human experience ought to have so vastly more weight than any scientific result."[98] Everyday experience, because it provides our concrete interaction with the indefinite richness of reality, founds the possibility of science and also provides the vague criterion of the shared meaningfulness and sense of workability of incommensurable scientific theories. Scientific knowledge is the paradigm for Peirce, not because he holds to scientific realism,[99] but because of the method by which scientific knowledge is achieved. The dynamics of science reflect and in turn help throw light upon the dynamics that give rise to the perceived world that founds the very possibility of science.

In the change of a scientific theory, according to Peirce, we apply methods and rules[100] whose operation cannot be subject to objective justifiability and eventual agreement. In accepting a theory for testing one incorporates such criteria as plausibility, simplicity, explanatory power, and economy.[101] And, as Nicholas Rescher's discussion of economy well indicates, there is a general, pervasive practice of economy in common sense that has not been achieved in science. As he states of the situation in general, "clever theoreticians" frequently "encounter perplexities to which the ordinary practitioner seems immune."[102] What holds of economy as well as other commonsense vague notions that form the backdrop for the highly criticizable claims of science holds as well for workability. Though the abstract articulations of workability and plausability[103] take diverse and at times incommensurable forms, both in science and in the more reflective questionings of common sense, the vague and acritically indubitable[104] sense of workability serves, ultimately, as the ineffable but inescapable and inexhaustible wellspring of vitality by which reasons and practices are worked out in the ongoing course of inquiry. And, as Peirce points out, workability is holistic in nature; observations do not determine the adjustments we make; workability is often best achieved by theories that are the most radically novel.[105]

When a community is operating within a common system of meanings on any one issue, then investigation can tend toward an ideal limit of convergence. However, when different segments of interpreters experience different facts because of different sets of meaning structures for cutting into the indefinitely rich continuity of possibilities of ordering, such convergence cannot occur. The criterion for adequately cutting is workability, but workability can be established only relative to some meaningful network by which experience is "caught." Thus there may be a plurality of interpretations among varying groups of interpreters on any topic. For each group, identifiable by varying nets or perspective for the catching of experience, is variously structuring some contours of a world. Yet even the lines of demarcation of distinct groups of interpreters are difficult to discern, for such differing networks are embodied in differing attitudes of response and may be present when disagreeing interpreters think their differences can be resolved merely "by collecting the facts." In this way, the essential pluralism is often hidden from view in the misplaced drive toward a common conclusion based on "the evidence."

Such pluralism must ultimately be dealt with in terms of a generalized stance of agreement concerning what standards are to be applied in making decisions among "incommensurable" frameworks for delineating facts. Such standards may be difficult to elucidate, but as implicitly operative they can be elicited for clarification. However, perspectives may emerge that not only are "incommensurable" with another conceptual net for the catching of experience through the determination of what kind of facts exist in the world, but also incorporate standards and criteria and solutional goals, or kinds of problems important to resolve, that are "incommensurable" with those of another perspective. Thus, there are not only different facts, but also different methods, standards, and criteria for determining which system of facts should be accepted. This is the most fundamental sense of incommensurability in Kuhn's position. These divergent perspectives have indeed carved out divergent worlds—be they divergent scientific worlds or divergent ways of life encompassing not just differing facts but differing goals, differing problems of importance, and differing criteria for resolving differences.

This deepest level of incommensurability, which has been shown by Kuhn to lie embedded in "the structure of scientific revolutions," leads to charges by his critics of irrationalism and the denial of progress in knowledge. Thus Skagestad, after a "piecemeal" flirtation with the linkage of Peirce with Kuhn via the questionable path indicated above, notes that "What is controversial is only whether such changes are progressive or arbitrary."[106] He concludes that Peirce, the realist, held the former, while Kuhn held the latter. Susan Haack similarly, but perhaps even more forcefully, distances Peirce from Kuhn here. Though acknowledging Peirce's recognition that historically growth in science sometimes progressed more cataclysmically than cumulatively, she is insistant that Peirce would have no sympathy for Kuhn's position of discontinuity and revolution in science and would have considered it to house a "covert commitment to nominalism."[107] The characterization of scientific progress for Peirce as radically opposed to the Kuhnsian position is perhaps brought home most forcefully in Resher's claim that Peirce holds a "cumulative-convergence" theory of scientific progress and that "Progress, on this view, consists in driving questions down to lesser and lesser magnitudes, providing increasingly enhanced detail of increasingly diminished significance. This at bottom is the Peircean vision of ultimate convergence in scientific inquiry."[108]

The denial of the alternatives and characterizations offered above by Skagestad, Haack, and Rescher requires a brief consideration of progress and rationality versus arbitrariness and irrationality as implicit in Peirce's writings. Peirce's position implicitly reveals the way in which the rational cannot be confined to what can be explicitly formulated in a series of propositions, for facts and their propositional formulations emerge from the backdrop of a world or a horizon of meaningful rapport that by its very nature cannot be brought to such formulation. At its most fundamental level it sets the precondition for the emergence for both doubt and conscious belief, for questioning cannot occur without the world as the context within which the doubt and questioning and possible solutions make sense. The function of "persuasion" in the "choice" of a world, however, does not involve a contrast between the rational and the non-rational but rather requires a new understanding of the nature of rationality. The irrationality of humans consists in "an exaggerated loyalty to their own principles"[109] rather than willingness to change in the light of the dynamics of scientific method. This method incorporates at all levels of its functioning the vague sense of workability and, as holistic in nature, is not reducible to rigid rules of procedure. Yet incommensurable perspectives, whether at the level of common sense or science, though in a sense structuring differing worlds, cannot, by the very nature of world as opening onto a natural universe with which we must successfully interact, be closed to rational discussion. In the ongoing course of experience some arguments or reasons gain vitality while others fall by the wayside. Though none are proved right or wrong, we "get over" some but yield to the force of others. Such a "getting over" or reinforcement is based on rational discussion, guided by a vague, elusive, but real sense of the inescapable criteria of workability. As Peirce well expressed the philosophic significance of such ongoing, ontologically grounded creativity, "we are neither forced into *idealism*, nor yet into *ontological ignorance*."[110] And thus Peirce appropriately held that his community of interpreters involves not a straight development but a self-corrective diversity of interpretations, abductive inferences, and arguments in constant process of adjustment as they interweave to form a fiber of understanding.[111]

Knowledge as cumulative and knowledge as changing do not lie in opposition for Peirce. Rather, knowledge as changing is also knowledge as cumulative, for any novel world emerges from a cumulative process or history, which yields enrichment of intelligibility both of the old and of the new. To demand of such a cumulative process that it tend toward a final unchanging truth is to misunderstand the nature of the indeterminately rich natural universe, the nature of noetic activity, and the nature of world within which both are unified. This unification undercuts the dichotomy of foundationalism or nonfoundationalism and, along with it, the closely related dichotomies of realism or anti-realism and objectivism or relativism, since each, in its own way, represents the alternatives of an absolute grounding of knowledge or skepticism. The present position provides an orientation within which these sets of alternatives do not apply. Experience incorporates an ontological intrusion as one aspect ingredient in it. Also ingredient in the very heart of human experience is an interpretive creativity that is at once unified with that ontological presence but renders its grasp in terms of any absolute grounding impossible. The unity denies the arbitrariness of anti-foundationalism or anti-realism, or relativism. The temporally founded creativity denies the absoluteness of foundationalism or realism or objectivism. Peirce's orientation provides a novel paradigm in which these popular but self-defeating dichotomies become irrelevant.

In one sense it can be said that the world within which conscious belief, questioning, and discussion emerge becomes many different worlds because of new meanings, shaping new worldly contours, that emerge from varying attitudes of response to developing problematic contexts. In another sense, however, such pluralism is not absolute but emerges within the backdrop of community. For, in its deepest sense, the questioning that changed the world could occur only within a context that did not change but lent the prereflective constancy and commonalty of its meaning in a general though vague sense to the meaningfulness of both the problematic contexts and the possible resolutions in terms of alternative structurings. It is the foundation for such a pluralistic community, rather than for the drive toward unanimity in final knowledge, that lies at the heart of Peirce's pragmatic position and provides the metaphysical and epistemic underpinnings for Kuhn's understanding of science.

These underpinnings reveal that Kuhn's understanding of the pluralistic nature of scientific change does not render such change arbitrary or irrational, nor does Peirce's understanding of scientific progress render such progress at odds with inherent pluralism. The deeply imbedded, pervasive strand of pragmatic pluralism that runs through Peirce's writings provides the foundation for the kinship of these two thinkers. It provides the epistemological and metaphysical tools for resolving many of the perplexities and dilemmas that have led to both the long held claims of their radical opposition as well as the recent piecemeal, halting attempts to effect a reconciliation. The following chapters will explore in detail these tools, some of which have been included in broad strokes in the above presentation, to reveal just how deeply and pervasively this strand of pluralism is embedded in Peirce's thought and how it weaves a unifying and clarifying pattern for understanding various of his claims and for providing an in-depth "new alternative."

CHAPTER 2

Meaning as Habit

Peirce's well-known pragmatic doctrine of meaning as habit permeates and helps illuminate the other intricately interwoven threads that constitute the pattern of his pragmatic pluralism. And the complex nature of this doctrine, as well as its significance for pluralism, can best be brought into focus via an issue that is usually considered quite "unpragmatic" and "un-Peircean," the analytic-synthetic distinction.

Peirce scholarship in general is implicitly pervaded by the assumption that the analytic-synthetic distinction is either denied by or irrelevant to Peirce's pragmatic empiricism. In 1965 Thomas Olshewsky argued that pragmatism in general precludes the bifurcation of statements into analytic propositions and synthetic propositions.[1] Three years later Robert Almeder argued that Peirce rejected the analytic-synthetic distinction, connecting this rejection with his acceptance of the fallibility of all knowledge, including the area of mathematics.[2] Later Peirce scholars have tended to take for granted Peirce's rejection of this bifurcation, with the result that the issue has been virtually ignored in recent literature.

In conjunction with this ongoing belief, there are recurring contexts of interpretation of Peirce's position that implicitly conflate his verificationalism as a theory of meaning and as a theory of truth, as well as his concept of habit as the basis of meaning and as the basis of belief. Thus, Manley Thompson, in rejecting reductionism, slides back and forth between "expressions of meaning" and "expressions of truth," and he concludes that although verificational meaning is reductionistic, Peirce avoids reductionism by "a still higher grade of clearness of thought," by ultimate meaning coming after verificational meaning has been given.[3] Bruce Altushuler, in his wide ranging discussion of Peirce's understanding of meaning, slides back and forth between meaning and truth, making no real distinction between habit as meaning and habit as belief.[4]

Within the context of these assumptions and ambiguities, there has emerged both a vigorous interest in Peirce's mathematical thought and a direct focus on his philosophy of science in terms of the contemporary importance of his recognition of the holistic aspects of scientific fallibilism. The following discussion will attempt to show that an examination of the way Peirce understands the certitude and specificity of mathematical truths implies the functioning of an analytic-synthetic distinction and that this in turn points toward an implicit yet pervasive and significant functioning of an analytic-synthetic distinction throughout empirical knowledge. This functioning provides the key for clearly distinguishing between the verificationalist dimensions of meaning and of truth and between the role of habit as the basis of meaning and the basis of belief. These features in turn point, in preliminary fashion, to his contextualistic and holistic approach to the nature of scientific fallibilism and to the possibility of an inherent pluralism in the very structuring of experience at all levels of awareness.[5] The following discussion will first turn to an overview of Peirce's understanding of mathematics in order to elicit those aspects of his thought that will be relevant to an understanding of his theory of meaning.

Peirce holds that mathematical truths are necessary truths in that mathematics draws conclusions that follow necessarily from their premisses.[6] There are two ways, however, in which mathematics does not provide certitude. First, the cognitive act of making a mathematical deduction may be mistaken. Thus, though one plus one necessarily yields a certain mathematical truth, and if I correctly add, then I have attained a necessary truth, yet it is not necessary that I add correctly, nor can I ever be absolutely certain that I have,[7] though in many ordinary mathematical calculations I can attain "practical infallibility."[8] Thus, Peirce can claim that while the business of the mathematician is to frame hypotheses and deduce from them necessary consequences,[9] yet such theoretical necessity does not parallel any cognitive infallibility, for such supposed infallibility appears only when viewed "through spectacles that cut off the rays of blunder." Because of this, "however improbable it may be, there is a certain finite probability that everyone who has ever performed this addition of 1 and 1 has blundered. . . . Looked at in this light, every mathematical inference is merely a matter of probability."[10] Thus, though there is a theoretical necessity attaching to correct mathematical conclusions, there is no theoretical infallibility, "a phrase that logical analysis proves to be a mere jingle of words with a jangle of contradictory meanings."[11] In brief, we can know that if we correctly grasp a mathematical truth, we have grasped a necessary truth; yet we can never know for certain that we have so correctly grasped one.

There is a second sense in which Peirce holds to a sort of "mathematical fallibility." Mathematics does not provide certitude about the world. Peirce here stresses that he does not mean that if pure hypotheses were to be true of an actual state of affairs, then the reasoning would cease to be necessary. Rather, one could never know apodictically that these hypotheses were true of an actual state of things.[12]

The starting points for mathematical reasonings are themselves neither necessary nor true. They are pure hypotheses asserting hypothetical states.[13] Thus, Peirce can say that:

> Kant regarded mathematical propositions as synthetical judgments a priori; wherein there is this much truth, that they are not, for the most part, what he called analytical judgments; that is, the predicate is not, in the sense he intended, contained in the definition of the subject.[14]

Thus, pure hypotheses, as indicating hypothetical states about which one may draw inferences, are themselves neither analytic nor synthetic. Mathematics is concerned neither with synthetic judgments nor with analytical judgments in Kant's sense, for the analytic certitude lies not in the subject predicate relation of the hypothesis but in the inferential relation of hypotheses to conclusions. There is a systematic theoretical analytic necessity based on containment, but there is no such necessity for a hypothetical starting point. Thus, a mathematical system is a system of necessarily related meanings such that the meanings set by the starting postulates necessarily contain that which they have the power to generate. "Everything (in mathematics) therefore, beyond the first precepts for the construction of the hypotheses, has to be of the nature of apodictic inference."[15] Or, in other terms, "The business of the mathematician is to frame an arbitrary hypothesis and then to deduce from this hypothesis such necessary consequences as can be drawn by diagrammatical reasoning."[16] This statement leads to the final relevant aspect of mathematical reasoning, its diagrammatical nature, a feature so fundamental for Peirce that he considers it his "first real discovery about mathematical procedure."[17]

Peirce makes a distinction between corollarial reasoning and theorematic reasoning, contrasting "trivial" corollarial reasoning with theorematic reasoning as diagrammatic. Diagrammatic or schematic[18] reasoning involves the introduction of an element of novelty in the deductive process, "through the formation in the imagination of some sort of diagrammatic, that is, iconic representation . . . as skeletonized as possible."[19] Though it is the aspect of iconic representation that is frequently stressed in discussions of Peirce's understanding of diagrammic reasoning, two key qualifications made by Peirce should be here observed. First, such a diagram involves both visual and muscular "imagery" by which it is seen that "the conclusion is compelled to be true by the conditions of the construction of the diagram."[20] Second, though he speaks of the formation of the diagrammic representation "in the imagination," he clarifies this by stressing that ultimately schematic structure is understood not as a generalization of imagined instances but as a product of a predictive rule.[21] Thus, the diagrammic reasoning of mathematics involves, ultimately, a predictive rule generative of the action-image matrix of a schematic structure. This schematic imagery allows for the introduction of novelty into mathematical reasoning; mere corollarial reasoning, or reasoning in general terms,[22] does not allow this, for the novelty of theorematic reasoning is attained by the construction of schematic imagery in which new relationships come to be recognized.

There has been a growing interest in the implications of Peirce's focus on the nature of theorematic reasoning as diagrammatic. On the one hand it has been argued that the diagrammatic nature of theorematic reasoning involves quantification,[23] while on the other hand it has been claimed that diagrammatic reasoning shows that mathematics is an experimental, hypothesis-confirming science in which one makes hypotheses about, and observes and experiments upon, diagrams according to a distinctive method.[24] According to the present interpretation, diagrammatic reasoning exemplifies the import of neither quantification nor experimental method but implicational or rule-generated relations—though this latter has important ramifications for understanding experimental method. Though it has been argued that the novelty involved in theorematic reasoning involves the introduction of novel postulates,[25] such novelty would seem to be best understood as the novelty of a creative construction for the discovery of what is already contained in or allowed by the starting point:

> It is necessary to set down, or to imagine, some individual and definite schema, or diagram. . . . This schema is constructed so as to conform to a hypothesis set forth in general terms in the thesis of the theorem. . . . After the schema has been constructed according to the precept virtually contained in the thesis . . . it is necessary that something should be DONE. . . . [P]ermissible transformations are made. Thereupon, the faculty of observation is called into play. Some relation between the parts of the schema is remarked. . . . Generally speaking, it may be necessary to draw distinct schemata to represent alternative possibilities.[26]

Mathematics, then, is a discipline that begins with creations of the mind, in themselves neither true nor false, and from them draws necessary conclusions, though one can never be sure that one has made the correct inference and has indeed reached a necessary conclusion. Such conclusions are necessary because they are "virtually contained" in the premises, though such containment comes to light only through the creativity of schematic thought, which brings to light novel relationships. Such schematic thought involves structures emerging through the interrelationship of predictive or generative rule, activity, and imagery. A series of schemata generated represents alternative possibilities of a predictive rule. The conditions of the construction of the schemata compel the truth of the conclusions.

In light of the above characterization of mathematical thought, the discussion can now turn to its relevance for Peirce's theory of meaning. The beginning of this relevance begins to emerge when Peirce, after carefully developing the position that theorematic reasoning, as opposed to corollarial reasoning, depends upon experimentation with individual schemata, concludes that "in the last analysis, the same thing is true of the corollarial reasoning too. . . . Only in this case, the very words serve as schemata."[27] Accordingly, the difference becomes not whether or not schemata are employed in the reasoning but whether the schemata are exemplified in words or are "specially constructed," the latter belonging to theorematical or mathematical reasoning proper. Moreover, to say that words are employed as schemata, for Peirce, would seem to indicate that meaning beneath the level of language employs schemata, for "meaning enters into language by determining it."[28] As Peirce summarizes the general significance of the diagrammatic reasoning of mathematics: "Icons have to be used in all thinking."[29] As he states more specifically of the pragmatist, he will "hold that everything in the substance of his beliefs can be represented by the schemata of his imagination."[30] The function of schemata embodied in commonsense perceptual awareness is expressed in Peirce's explanation that

> The Diagram remains in the field of perception or "imagination" and so the Iconic Diagram and its initial Symbolic interpretant taken together constitute what we shall not too much wrench Kant's term in calling a schema, which is on the one side an object capable of being observed, while on the other side it is a general.[31]

It will be seen below that Peirce's pragmatic appropriation of Kantian schemata within the structure of meaning embodies a logical truth that can be understood in terms of the characteristics of mathematical thought. That mathematics should provide the best understanding of this logical truth is perhaps to be expected, for logical truth is "grounded on a sort of observation of the same kind as that upon which mathematics is grounded. For this reason, it is desirable at once to examine the nature of the mathematician's procedure pretty thoroughly."[32]

It will further be seen that Peirce, in appropriating Kantian schemata, takes from Kant the fundamental insight that concepts are empirically meaningful only if they contain schematic possibilities for their application to sensible experience. Further, the imagery that makes possible the application of a concept cannot be abstracted out from sense experience but must be provided before meaningful perceptual content can emerge within experience. However, Peirce's pragmatic appropriation of these insights radically alters Kant's understanding of the schema. Such a schema is no longer a product of productive imagination as distinct from the understanding as the faculty of judgment. Rather, both understanding and imagination are unified and transformed into a creative functioning of habit as providing a lived or vital intentionality between knower and known. Such an interactional unity of knower and known, rooted in the human mode of existing in the world in terms of purposive activity, is incorporated within the internal structure of meaning through the functioning of Peirce's unique appropriation of Kantian schemata.[33] Peirce's pragmatic stress on meaning in terms of habits of response is, of course, well known.[34] However, the language in which it is usually expressed tends too often to conflate its epistemic and ontological dimensions,[35] thereby hiding from view its full systematic significance. The following discussion will provide a brief sketch of Peirce's analysis of meanings as epistemic relational structures that embody the characteristics of a deductive system in their very internal structure.

It is frequently asserted, in rejecting the phenomenalist alternative in general and, more particularly, in rejecting interpretations of Peirce's position as a type of phenomenalism, that phenomenalistic expressions presuppose and are parasitic upon physical-object language. Thus, the logic of language is held to show that Peirce cannot be consistently read as a phenomenalist.[36] At the linguistic level one indeed does find such an antiphenomenalistic logic of language. However, such an assertion in defense of pragmatism does not utilize the full force of the Peirce's rejection of phenomenalism,[37] since it does not adequately ground the issue in its epistemic roots. For Peirce, the epistemic import of such a logic of language lies in the fact that it incorporates the dynamics of lived experience at its most rudimentary level, a dynamics that in turn reflects a semiotic structure operative at its most fundamental level. The significance of the logic of language lies in the fact that it grounds itself in those most rudimentary semiotic structures by which humans experience a world of appearing objects. Hence, an examination of such epistemic foundations should lay bare the basis for the logic of linguistic structure.

For Peirce, meanings are to be understood as logical structures,[38] not as psychological or biological facts. Peirce does not want to give meaning an existence independent of purpose, yet he does not want to reduce meaning to the categories of psychology or biology.[39] Meanings are to be understood, for Peirce, as relational structures emerging from behavioral patterns, as emerging from the lived-through response of the human organism to that universe with which it is in interaction. Or, in other terms, human behavior is meaningful behavior, and it is in behavior that the relational patterns that constitute conceptual meaning are rooted. What, however, is meaning as a relational pattern? A purely relational pattern devoid of sensuous criteria of recognition would be a pattern of relationships relating nothing that had reference to the world, while a pure datum, devoid of the relational pattern, could not be an object of thought. For Peirce, sensuous recognition and conceptual interpretation represent two ends of a continuum rather than an absolute difference in kind. His view that sensuous recognition involves interpretive aspects, in some yet to be determined sense, is fairly clear-cut and can be found in his view that there are no first impressions of sense.[40] However, Peirce's view that conceptualization requires imagery is open to some confusion. He states that "I will go so far as to say that we have no images even in actual perception."[41] Yet, he objects to Kant, not because Kant requires a schema for the application of a concept to experience, but because he separates the schema from the concept, failing to recognize that a schema for the application of a concept to the data of experience is as general as the concept.[42] And, if the schema is to allow for the application of a concept to sense experience, then imagery, in some sense at least, would seem to be required.

The resolution of this difficulty lies in the definition of image that Peirce so emphatically rejects in the former statement, that is, the definition of image as an absolutely singular representation, a representation absolutely determinate in all respects.[43] Thus, Peirce accepts imagery as part of conceptual meaning, but he refuses to equate imagery with determinate, singular representation. In the schematic aspect of conceptual meaning, then, there would seem to be found the inseparable mingling of the sensuous and the relational as the vehicle by which we think about and recognize objects in the world.[44]

This mingling can best be understood in terms of the relation between habit and schematic structure.[45] Such a relation emerges only in unifying Peirce's unsystematic analyses found scattered throughout his writings, for Peirce did not recognize until late in his career that in addition to his carefully worked out logical analysis of the sign process, or relation between representamen, interpretant, and object, his philosophy required a similarly worked out analysis of the internal structure of the concept or logical interpretant. As Peirce stated in a letter written toward the end of his life, "I shall undertake to show that concepts are capable of such phaneroscopic analysis, or, in common parlance 'logical analysis'; but there are only a few cases in which I pretend as yet to carry the analysis so far as to resolve the concept into its ultimate elements."[46] Such brief and unsystematic analyses found throughout his writings, when brought to a systematic development in terms of his overall pragmatic position, reveal both the emergence of meanings as precise logical structures and the deeply rooted rejection of the phenomenalist alternative, and they lead directly to the analysis of the logical interpretant.

The term *interpretant* refers to an effect produced in the interpreter by a sign.[47] The logical interpretant is a concept[48] and is the only interpretant "properly denominated a concept."[49] Furthermore, such intellectual concepts, which are, properly speaking, the only kind of concept there is, are "those upon the structure of which arguments concerning objective fact may hinge."[50] Thus far, then, it would seem that the logical interpretant is a concept in the interpreter that can have reference to objective fact. And, ultimately, the concept must be understood in terms of a habit of response.[51] To say, however, that a meaning or a concept is a habit of response in an interpreter seems somewhat inadequate for a position that places so much stress on both the interrelation of meaning and logic[52] as well as the dissociation of meaning and psychology.[53]

Peirce held that conceptual meaning must include within itself the emotional, energetic, and logical interpretants or, in other terms, the elements of Firstness, Secondness, and Thirdness found, in some form, in all analyses; in this case: Firstness as feeling core or sensuous content; Secondness as response or set of acts; and Thirdness as structure or resultant image. There is a disagreement between Murray Murphy and Bruce Altushuler as to whether Peirce's sense of meaning involves characters or actions, and Altushuler is led to distinguish in Peirce's philosophy two senses of meaning, corresponding to each of these two features.[54] According to the present interpretation, there are not two distinct senses of meaning, nor are the two features of character and action separable, for they are inseparably interwoven through the functioning of habit as productive rule. Imagery, then, as part of the internal structure of meaning, is inseparably connected with sense content as Firstness and pattern of reaction as Secondness.[55] As Peirce observes, "To predicate a concept of a real or imaginary object is equivalent to declaring that a certain operation, corresponding to the concept, if performed upon that object would . . . be followed by a result of a definite general description."[56] Or, in other terms,

"How otherwise can a habit be described than by a description of the kind of action to which it gives rise, with the specification of the conditions and the motive?"[57]

Here it should be noted that it is habit that gives rise to certain kinds of action in the presence of certain kinds of conditions to yield certain kinds of results. The relation among possible conditions, acts, and results is presented in the very structure of the logical interpretant as the resultant intended objective structure. And, if the act is dependent upon the condition or sensory content, then different sensory conditions will give rise to different acts. For example, varying perspectives of an object lead one to varying reactions. Even if one considers only one essential property, so that the application of the physical object concept is determined solely by the presence of one property, the use of test routine leads to an unlimited number of possible tests. Thus, there is not one act but an indefinite number of possible acts corresponding to an indefinite number of possible cues or sensory appearances. Yet, this indefinite number of cues and acts must lead to one resultant structure or conceptual object. Precisely what it means to see an object or objective structure rather than an appearance only is to "fill in" the resulting appearance of a particular act with the results of other possible acts, given other possible cues. Thus, in a sense there are an indefinite number of cues, acts, and resultant appearances. Yet, in another sense, though there are an indefinite number of cues and acts, they are all "part of" the one result, an objective conceptual structure having certain characteristics. The difference between an apprehended appearance and an apprehended object, for Peirce, is precisely this difference in levels of interpretation or conceptual organization. Any objectivity indicates an indefinite number of possible qualitative appearances.

Thus, if we are meaningfully to assert the existence of physical objects, or, in other terms, to organize experience via physical object concepts, then there must be, in addition to sensory cue, act, and further sensory appearance, that which binds into a system the set of possible sensory cues and possible resultant acts that as a system give rise to the resultant objective structure. Here it is necessary to distinguish between the logical interpretant, or resultant schematic structure, and the ultimate logical interpretant as the living habit that binds together into a systematic unity the various possibilities, thus making the logical interpretant possible. The concrete meaning, as the disposition or habit, is the source of the generation of explicit schemata, each of which makes precise for conscious awareness some aspect of the concrete meaning, some selection from the inexhaustible range of possibilities.

Conceptual meaning thus includes the total set of possible appearances and possible transformations via appropriate responses to other appearances as controlled by habit as a rule of generation and organization. This dispositional rule fills in a resultant schematic appearance with the results of other possible acts given other possible conditions, thereby providing "intentional objectivity." Thus, what is apprehended is not an appearance only but a perspective of an object. It has been rightfully noted that "A habit does not fully determine actual behavior; under different circumstances, it leaves open different possibilities or means of reaching certain goals."[58] However, it is habit that generates and unifies the range of possibilities of kinds of action given kinds of conditions in achieving the object or intended "goal;" for habit binds into a system the set of possible conditions and possible acts that as a system gives rise to the intended objective structure. As Peirce states, "to say that mental phenomena are governed by law" means that "there is a living idea" that pervades mental phenomena.[59]

These, then, are the "elements" or "ingredients" that interact to give rise to the logic of conceptual structure. The significance of the generality of all aspects of the schema, however, remains to be examined. And here it must be noted that for Peirce habit does more than unify three preexistent elements—sensory cues, acts, and resultant structure. Only as habit performs its function of unifying sensory cue and reaction does structure emerge at all. As Peirce states, "the general idea is the mark of the habit."[60] Furthermore, and perhaps even more significant for the present examination, habit determines reaction, and reaction partially determines the nature of the sensory cue. Thus habit ultimately partially determines the nature of the sensory cue. As Peirce notes, "feeling which has not yet emerged into immediate consciousness is already affectible and already affected. In fact, this is habit."[61]

Thus, not only is the conceptual objectivity fixed in its character through the functioning of habit in "filling in" the results of an act with the results of other possible acts, given other possible cues, but the appearance that is apprehended by a withholding of this "filling in" is itself partially fixed in its character precisely by that which is being "withheld." Pure "feeling core," pure Firstness, or pure "sense content" is "there" in experience as the logically or epistemically final basis and ultimate referent for all cognitive activity. In this sense it is epistemically primitive. Further, such a "feeling core" held apart from particular experiences must be "there" as part of the schema if concepts are to be applicable to experience. But, it is not isolatable in its purity; it is not, in its purity, apprehended appearance.[62] However, appearances, with their core of sensuous content, are the bedrock data to which one can work back in conscious awareness and the bedrock data to which one can appeal in the verification, through immediate passages of experience, of the application of conceptual meanings to the data of experience. In brief, immediate experience is not the experience of pure immediacy; it is shot through with the dispositional structure orderings of objectivity, for the appearances apprehended in "immediate experience" are generated indirectly through the functioning of habit. They are, in brief, a "mediated immediacy."[63]

Peirce's position can perhaps best be clarified by taking the term *image* as *aspect*. For example, one may say, quite correctly, that an ocean presents a turbulent image or aspect. And, while the specific empirical content of experience is best understood as one particular among many, the schema for the application of a living meaning or habit to experience is best understood as the one that determines the many. Indeed, the importance of the content of the schematic structure lies in the way in which it comes into being. Such a structure represents an aspect of the dispositional structure order that regulates it and that governs the possible transformations from one schematic aspect to another. As in mathematical schemata, "the diagram is modified in some manner already shown to be possible"[64] Thus, the series of possible schemata for the application of a concept to experience is "fixed" prior to the imposition of a linguistic structure. Yet, it is "fixed" not by any eternal ontological order but by the concrete, biologically based disposition or habit as the rule of generation of explicit schemata. Such habit cannot be reduced to the "merely psychological," for what it binds together into a unity is a triadic relationship of factors emerging from organism-environment interaction. Thus, meanings emerge from organism-environment interaction as precise triadic relational structures unified by habit as a rule of organization and as a rule of generation of specific schemata, and it is only within the backdrop of such a functioning that appearances come to awareness.[65]

A schematic structure representing an aspect of an ordering cannot be reduced to the content of any experience, whether imagined or actual. Instead, it represents principles or possibilities in terms of which sensory content can emerge within experience. The core of sensuous content or Firstness that forms the basis of imagery is precisely what Peirce elsewhere calls the "ponecipuum"[66] or logically primitive criterion of recognition of immediately felt sensory content which, though it serves as the "particular stimulus" within the logic of concepts, is itself an epistemic universal that has been determined at a more fundamental level. Schematic structure, then, forms, at all levels, a principle or rule of interpretation of particulars as opposed to the manifold of particulars delineated or organized by it.

Thus, meaning as habit is a rule for the production of schematic aspects as the conditions for possible verifying instances.[67] The living meaning "virtually contains"[68] the conditions for its verification. Such conditions are not collections of actual or possible verifying instances; rather, they consist of the relational generality of schematic aspects that set the conditions of recognition for what will count as verifying instances. The if-then orderings of such general relations or conditional resolutions to action[69] are analytically contained in the perceptual meaning. Not only does meaning as dispositional contain an indefinite number of possible kinds of verification in respect to possible kinds of conditions, but each kind is itself a generality that, rather than a collection of possible verifying instances, helps give structure to such instances. As a "kind," it is analytically contained in, or is part of, a meaning, while an instance of a kind, delineated by such meaning, gives evidence for the applicability of the meaning. Thus, meaning is in principle irreducible to verifying instances, actual or possible,[70] because possible conditions of verification, contained in the meaning, are different in their very nature from any number of particular verifying instances, actual or possible.[71] To clarify further the way in which meaning as a dispositional rule of generation of schematic forms of possible verifications is irreducible in principle to actual and possible verifying instances, it is necessary to further clarify the way the logical interpretant, as schematic mark of the habit, and the ultimate logical interpretant, as dispositional rule, are linked by the relation of generation.

Dispositions cannot be said to generate explicit schemata in the sense of providing a copy—even a partial one. A schema is not a particular copy of a general rule. It is not a copy of anything; nor, as shown above, is anything in the schema particular. The most adequate model to indicate the relationship of disposition to schematic structure is precisely that of a mathematical rule generating a number series or, as Peirce often explicitly develops it, of a continuity containing an infinite number of possible cuts.[72] A mathematical rule of generation cannot be separated from that which it generates, for that which is generated represents an aspect of the structural order by which it is generated. In understanding the relational structure of that which is generated, we understand to that extent the rule that generates it. The disposition or ground of meaning cannot, it is true, be inspected an sich, but it is inspectable in any aspect. Explicit aspects can be continually generated for inspection, though the rule of generation will never be exhausted by the schemata and hence can never in principle be completely inspected.

A disposition is concrete, and any attempt to make it clear and explicit requires an abstraction from this concreteness.[73] That the total concrete meaning as a disposition cannot be made fully explicit is undeniable. As Peirce points out, "A disposition or kind of behavior . . . is not in all respects determinate."[74] This, however, does not lead to a fourth kind of meaning, which saves verificational meaning from leading Peirce into reductionism,[75] for "concrete reasonableness" is not a fourth kind of meaning but the very basis of meaning as verificational. It is that living concrete habit that is the source of schematic forms of possible types of verifying instances. For this reason, a meaning is never fully determinate but always further determinable.

Further, the concreteness of living habit provides the conceptual counterpart of the "that which has" characteristics, and the "that which has" can never be exhausted by the qualitative lawfulness that it incorporates. And, as representing a "that which has," or a possible existent individual, there is a further indeterminateness, for schematic forms of dispositional meaning not only reveal that certain structural and qualitative characteristics are included in the very meaning of the intended object and are, in fact, criteria for delineating that kind of object within experience, but also further reveal that indefinite numbers of characteristics are not essential. An object as a concrete individual contains not just those characteristics necessary for its being a particular type of object, but also the indefinite specificity of having or not having other characteristics. Concrete meanings represent an object to which essential characteristics must apply and to which nonessential characteristics may or may not apply. Peirce holds that "No concepts, not even those of mathematics, are absolutely precise."[76] Further, no individual, in its concrete individually, can be precisely grasped. For example, "When I see a thing, I do not see that it is not sweet, nor do I see that it is sweet; and therefore, what I see is capable of logical division into the sweet and the not sweet."[77] Thus, the specificity of meaning that lies in the disposition or habit as the rule of generation includes within itself a basic indeterminateness both in relation to the total meaning and in relation to the specificity of the concrete, existing object denoted.

For Peirce, meaning is indeterminate in that there is in principle always more to specify. And, its application to the world is further indeterminate in that its very meaning intends that to which the attribution of a limitless number of nonessential characteristics is always possible.[78] Here it must be stressed that this difference between the concreteness of an existing object and a set of qualities is not the difference between extension and intension. Rather, the intensional meaning contains the meaningfulness of the concreteness of objectivity or "existence" as that which can never be reduced to a set of qualitative aspects or structural relations, for quality is Firstness, and structural relation is Thirdness, while the "that which has" qualities and relations manifests Secondness, or the concreteness of existence, and this concreteness is built into the very meaning intended. Thus, meaning identifies an individual existence as an instance of a kind, not as a uniquely concrete individual, yet it also provides the meaningful recognition that concrete individuality provides an "always more." We can denote objects rather than collections of qualities because our meanings embody the basis of the concreteness of objectivity, of concrete existence, of the "that which incorporates" certain lawful modes of behavior and certain qualitative possibilities. The ultimate logical interpretant, as living habit, thus provides the meaning of the dynamical bond.[79]

In no respect, then, is the intentional meaning of dispositions reducible to the denotation of verifying instances. Both a "this" as an apprehension of a thing and a "this" as an apprehension of an appearance or a character are embedded within the structure of dispositional meaning as intensional. The very concreteness of the "this" as that which has certain characteristics is incorporated within the concreteness of habit as the "living meaning."[80] The meaning of the concreteness of reacting Secondness embodying qualitative lawful continuities is included in the concreteness of habit as rule, and it is represented in the perspectival aspect of schematic structure. Thus, perceptual meaning is an organization of characters by which one intends the meaning of an object as that to which essential properties must apply[81] and to which nonessential properties may or may not apply, and these two types of applicability are built into the very sense of, or the meaning of, the concepts by which we delineate a world of perceptual objects. This meaning must be prior to the very possibility of denotable instances.

What the above discussion of generative rule indicates is that the fundamental concept for analyticity for Peirce is not synonymy but containment. Though analyticity is usually treated in terms of synonymy,[82] Peirce states that he was "led to the copula of inclusion," but he objects to the copula of identity.[83] As he puzzled over the problem of containment:

> Consider a state of mind which is a conception. It is a conception by virtue of having a meaning, a logical comprehension; and if it is applicable to any object, it is because that object has the characters contained in the comprehension of this conception. Now the logical comprehension of a thought is usually said to consist of the thoughts contained in it, but thoughts are events.[84]

Peirce finds the answer to the puzzle in the distinction between the concrete disposition or habit as the rule of organization and the awareness of the schematic aspects of that which is organized by the rule. Thus, through the internal logic of the functioning of meaning as dispositional, Peirce can offer a solution to the problem of containment. It is through an understanding of this internal functioning that we can understand the sense in which one can discover that some quality or character is essential to the meaning in question. Such a discovery requires "a real effective force behind consciousness," or, in other terms, a living habit.[85] Similarly, this functioning of meaning makes clear the way in which a meaning of which one is not conscious may be implicit in that meaning of which one is conscious. Thus Peirce holds that "the meaning of a thought is something altogether virtual." It "lies not in what is actually thought, but in what this thought may be connected with in representation by subsequent thoughts."[86] Indeed, how the meaning implicit in behavior becomes explicit and what would be recognized as essential when the meaning is examined is already implicit in the dispositional mode of response.

In this way, we can understand a habit through "an experiment in the imagination,"[87] one that brings to awareness a schematic aspect. As Peirce concludes, "What we must mean, therefore, by saying that one concept is contained in another, is that we normally represent one to be in the other, that is, that we form a particular kind of judgment, or which the subject signifies one concept and the predicate the other."[88] Such a "particular kind of judgment" would seem to be an analytic judgment,[89] which expresses a deductive relation of containment between generative rule and schematic product. And, what follows from this is that some judgments that we do not recognize to be analytic may be so—not that those we recognize to be so cannot be. Such analytic judgments express necessary truths, though they need not be exhaustive of the meaning. Further, we can never have theoretical certitude that we have correctly grasped an analytic truth, though if we have correctly grasped, then what we have grasped is a necessary truth. Here Peirce's radical fallibilism, which holds that we can not only miss but be wrong about analytic truths, presents a strong challenge to contemporary assumptions.

Important meaning structures may be difficult to capture by tracing which concepts are included in which in an explicit articulation of a relationship. But explicit articulation of the analysis of a concept is ultimately an attempt to capture what has implicitly been operative in the structure of our habits, a structure that contains the schematic forms of the concept. This behavioral containment is for Peirce the foundation for the explicit articulation of analytic claims, regardless of how difficult the explicit articulation may be or what form it may take. This behavioral level in an important sense undercuts some of the contemporary debates about the nature of analytic truths as articulated in explicit claims.

That mathematical thought forms the model for such analyticity is again indicated by Peirce's assertion that

> I was much occupied by the question whether or not a notation similar to this [notation useful in the analytic presentation of theorems in geometry] would not represent the modes in which concepts are, or should be, represented as compounded in definition, with a leaning to the affirmative.[90]

Mathematics, because of its analytic nature,[91] tells us about a general range of possibility but in itself gives us "no positive knowledge, no knowledge of what actually is;" yet Peirce further holds that knowledge that excludes this element could not provide us with knowledge "relating to a whole general range of possibility."[92]

It has been claimed above that for Peirce a meaning is analogous to a mathematical deductive system, incorporating an analyticity based on the concept of containment. However, the starting point of a mathematical deduction is itself purely hypothetical, while our empirical meanings are inherently related to experience. Meanings arise from experience and are in turn verified by experience. The above analysis leaves unexplained this basic relatedness to experience. Peirce, in seeking an explanation, puzzled concerning the applicability of mathematics: "How comes it that the conclusion is applicable whenever the premise is applicable?"[93]

Also, at this point, related objections may be raised. First, how can such a "fixity" to meanings take account of the functionalism of attitudes or response, of the way in which our meanings are continually open to revision, of the social nature of meaning? Peirce of course stresses both the communal aspects of meanings and the revisability of meanings. Second, it may be objected that the meaning of the real generality of the if-then conditionals of act-result relations has been maintained only at the expense of fallibilism. It has been claimed that the if-then of the conditional can be understood as contrary to fact because it is part of the general, rule-generated meaning and as such is irreducible to actual or possible verifying instances. And, if these "conditional resolutions to action" are contained in the meaning, then, though verifying instances cannot prove necessarily the applicability of a meaning, it would seem that a disconfirming instance can prove necessarily the inapplicability of a meaning through the operation of modus tolens. Thus, it would seem that though the truth of claims asserting the applicability of a concept to experience is probabilistic, the claim denying the applicability of a concept is certain. These types of objections lead from the logical conditions of meaning to the empirical conditions of truth and from habit as the basis of meaning to habit as the basis of belief. These issues in turn must be approached in terms of both the genesis of meanings and the structure of their verification.

The inherent relatedness to experience of our empirical meanings leads to the objection that structures so rich in empirical meaning can arise neither through arbitrary definition nor through stipulation, as in mathematics. However, the "fixation" of such structures corresponds to neither of these alternatives. It arises through the fixation of a set of experienced relationships unified by habit as a rule of organization. The fixation intended corresponds most closely to the creative process that Peirce calls "abduction," though what are here fixed by such creative activities or abductive processes are not empirical hypothesis asserting the applicability of meanings but the very structure of the meanings themselves. As Peirce states, "An abduction is Originary in respect to being the only kind of argument which starts a new idea."[94] And, habit, as creatively structuring, always brings a "more than" to the organization of past experiences, though it is these past experiences that in fact "nourished" the habit in which they are now contained.[95]

Israel Scheffler's assumption that Peirce's pragmatic maxim is similar to Bridgman's operational definition, in which meaning is reducible to verifying instances and in which the "more than" disappears, underlies his claim that Peirce must deny the validity of theoretical structures in science.[96] Almeder rightfully notes that for Peirce the meaning of a physical theory is underdetermined by observation data.[97] However, it has been seen that so also is perceptual meaning or perceptual "theory." Perceptual objects are "theory-laden" in the sense that they are constituted via the meanings through which we perceive our world and that we have brought to our world. Perceptual meanings are theoretical in the sense that they are the explanations or interpretations by which that which is there reveals itself to us.

Genetically, our meanings arise through the cumulative effect of past experience and the abductive, creative fixation, within the ongoing course of experience, of dispositionally organized relationships among experiences. But at any point in the knowledge process, the meaning logically contains all that it has creatively fixated or, conversely, all that it now has the power or potential to generate. The meanings embodied in our conceptual schemes are built up in the light of past experience. They are drawn from the empirical situation, although the relation among the meanings is statable apart from any particular instance of fact. The origin of our analytic structures, then, is empirical, pragmatic, functional. This genesis of meanings from the context of experience is in no way analogous to the logical reducibility of meanings to experience. The first answers the question as to why we create the meanings we do; the second answers the question as to what a meaning is. Meaning, qua created structure, contains no truth claim as to applicability in experience. Though for pragmatic reasons we must create or abductively fixate meanings with workable applications in the ongoing course of experience, a meaning itself is a deductive system applying to a hypothetical state of affairs, the implications of which we can know about since we create it.[98] Fred Michael claims that while Kant held that the mind imposes a schema of its own devising upon experience, Peirce's position is that the mind derives from experience the schema it imposes.[99] The present position is that the mind devises the schema as its creative, imaginative product, yet its creativity is guided by the pragmatic need to grasp experience in workable ways.

Peirce states of a geometrical diagram that it conveys "no positive or factual information; for it affords no assurance that there is any such thing in nature. But it is of the utmost value for enabling its interpreter to study what would be the character of such an object in case any such did exist."[100] If that which a meaning generates, or in other terms, contains, is too frequently inapplicable, our meaning may alter through the formation of new habits that creatively fixate inductively accumulated experiences in new ways. But what we then have is a new meaning, or a new rule of generation of conditions of verification, which now necessarily contains at least partially different schematic possibilities. Meanings do not literally change; rather, a new meaning replaces an old meaning. Though the same words may be used, there is a substitution of the meanings or concepts attached to them.[101] "Such words as force, law, wealth, marriage, bear for us very different meanings from those they bore to our barbarous ancestors."[102] For Peirce, "A self-contradictory proposition is not meaningless; it means too much."[103] It "means" something in the predicate, not allowed by the subject as the dispositional rule of generation. However, through a change of meanings, though not necessarily of words, what is inconceivable today may become conceivable tomorrow.[104]

Before one can make empirical generalizations about facts, one must have delineated facts through meanings that are prescriptive for what experiences will constitute the experience of particular kinds of facts. Before one can make the empirical claim that a particular kind of fact is "there," one must have the structure of the experiences that are to count as exemplifications of the presence of a particular kind of fact. Thus, the analytic structures of meanings provide the tools without which synthetic statements about the nature of experience cannot be made. Yet, these tools themselves are fashioned in the light of the cumulative effects of past experience through the abductive "fixation" of experienced uniformities. This is not a vicious circle but a cumulative process based on the pragmatic interplay at all levels between concepts and experience.

The way in which any conceptual structure originates genetically in experience but is yet logically or epistemically prior to the delineation of what is presented in any particular experience reflects the difference between the indefinite extendability of the interpretive process as a whole and the unity and completeness of any one particular interpretive structure or concept. Genetically the interpretive process can be extended indefinitely, for the cumulative knowledge process is unending; our concepts, based on previous experiences delineated by previous concepts, become more and more sophisticated. Yet, at any point in the cumulative knowledge process, a particular conceptual structure is complete and self-sufficient; it has an internal unity that requires nothing beyond itself for its fulfillment.

This interrelation of the absoluteness of intensional relationships of meanings and the functionalism of response as the determining factor in the fixation of meanings is concisely indicated by Peirce in his discussion of the fourth of four different kinds of uniformity and nonuniformity that may influence our reasoning:

> An object may have more or less tendency to possess the whole of certain sets of characters when it possesses any of them.
>
> A consideration of this sort may be so strong as to amount to demonstration of the conclusion. In this case, the inference is mere deduction—that is, the application of a general rule already established. In other cases, the consideration of uniformities will not wholly destroy the inductive or hypothetic character of the inference, but will only strengthen or weaken it by the addition of a new argument of a deductive kind.[105]

In brief, and in part conversely stated, the meaning of an object contains analytically a set of interrelated characteristics structured according to the established dispositional rule. However, if such relationships are not applicable to the experienced uniformities, such inductively established inapplicability may lead to the formation of a new meaning as the abductive or hypothetic "explanation" of the uniformities.

The origin of meaning systems partially constitutive of perceptual experience may help in solving Peirce's puzzlement concerning the applicability of mathematics. The logical structure of mathematics explains what mathematics is; however, why it is applicable concerns the issue of how our cumulative past experience leads to the abductive fixation of certain particular types of meaning structures. Accumulation of experience may lead to new empirical generalizations about facts or objects, but it can also lead to meaning replacements, to new facts or new objects. This, however, leads directly to the problem of verification of empirical judgments asserting the applicability of a meaning[106] or, conversely, asserting its inapplicability through the non-fulfillment of verifying instances.

As stated above, if the conditional resolutions to action are analytically contained in the meaning, then, though verifying instances cannot prove with certitude the applicability of the meaning[107] that generates them, it may yet seem that a disconfirming instance can prove with certainty its inapplicability by the operation of modus tolens. An examination of the structure of meaning has indeed shown that the generality of essential verification conditions expressable in counterfactual statements is contained in the meaning. However, what the genesis of meaning has shown is that what is asserted as holding counterfactually are probability relations, not exceptionless uniformities. Real relations are not held by

Peirce to require perfect correlations. It is false "that the ordinary and usual course of nature never can be broken through."[108]

What habit creatively structures is a set of inductively learned probabilistic relations expressable, via meanings, as the generality of forms of verification. Thus, the contrary-to-fact conditionals express probabilistic relations. As Peirce succinctly summarizes, the words *probably about* can indicate the modality in which a conclusion is drawn. But they can also be considered "as forming part of the contents of the conclusion; only from that point of view the inference ceases to be probable, and becomes rigidly necessary."[109] Thus, the contrary-to-fact conditionals contained in the dispositional meaning express probabilistic relations. The meaning necessarily implies that if act A is performed, result B will in all probability follow. If B does follow, then there is partial verification of the meaning applicability. However, if B does not follow, there is again only partial disconfirmation of the applicability of the meaning, for no one instance in experience can disprove a probability claim. There are two different levels of probability involved in the above structure of verification. Verifying instances give evidence for the probability of there being a real probability relation. What is being held probably to exist is a real relation that itself is characterized as a probability relation. What is confirmed by verifying instances is the probability that a real probability relation exists. Conversely, disconfirming instances increase the probability that no such probability relation does, in fact, exist.

Experience of an expected occurrence verifies, though never completely, the applicability of the if-then of real connection, the generality of which is contained in the meaning, and thus it helps to verify, indirectly, the applicability of the meaning. Accumulations of instances of such verifications provide the ground for, or the basis of, habits of belief and contingent, probabilistic, but often practically undoubted, perceptual claims or abductive hypotheses.[110] The purpose of the creation of perceptual meanings is the establishment of true beliefs which allow for successful interaction with a surrounding universe. Thus, such meanings are structured in the light of cumulative experience, and their applicability is verified by confirming experiences. However, there is a theoretically sharp distinction between analytic judgments about the conditions of verification contained in a meaning and synthetic or empirical judgments about the applicability of an empirical meaning to a segment of experience or about a relation claimed to hold, within experience, between distinct meanings.

Yet, though there is such a theoretically sharp distinction, all knowledge is fallibilistic and contextualistic. Just as all empirical generalizations are subject to error, so the empirical claim of the applicability of a meaning to a segment of experience is always fallible. Both are examples of contingent truths, fallible knowledge. So, also, our explications of meanings, though yielding necessary truths if correctly made, are always subject to error, thus providing only fallible knowledge about necessary truths. The very claim that a relationship between meanings is in fact analytic or synthetic is itself always fallible; we may easily, through failure of analysis, take as synthetic a relation that is in fact analytic. And, when experience turns out unexpectedly, requiring a change in our set of beliefs, there is no certainty as to whether experience has overturned an empirical generalization only or has given rise, on pragmatic grounds, to a new meaning.[111] We can never be certain if and when a highly confirmed empirical generalization about an object becomes incorporated into the very meaning of the object, related necessarily to the dispositional rule that now has the power to generate it. The cumulative effects of experience can lead to new empirical generalizations about the same meaningful contents of experience, or they can lead to the perception of different contents by the replacement of the meanings in terms of which contents of a particular type can emerge within experience.

As was developed in a different context in the previous chapter, we test beliefs not in isolation but as parts of a whole set of claims.[112] Something similar to auxiliary hypothesis in science is operative in our commonsense awareness of the world around us. No part of a relevant corpus of knowledge is immune from change in the face of repeated disconfirming instances. And any part of a belief structure can be held in the face of disconfirming evidence by changing other parts of the structure.[113] Experience reveals that an improvement is necessary, but clearly not which improvement is needed. Whether we change empirical generalizations in the face of disconfirming evidence or restructure a set of meanings that does not adequately capture experience is not itself dictated by the evidence; it is a pragmatic decision operative within the context of that encompassing intensional unity of humans and nature. Furthermore, experience usually proceeds without any awareness as to whether or not we have modified an empirical generalization by counterinstances or have replaced a meaning to avoid having to "throw out" too much of experience as not real contents of a particular type, for such "pragmatic decisions" are implicit in modes of response.

At this point, it may be asked whether, after such a long excursion, the only conclusion to be reached after all is that the supposed distinction between analytic meaning containments and empirical generalizations within Peirce's philosophy is nebulous at best, totally useless at worst. The answer here is a decided no. This sharp theoretical difference, which is always operative within the structure of knowledge, though always elusive for our recognition because of its fallibilistic, holistic, contextualistic features, shows that for Peirce there is rooted at the very basis of lived experience as pragmatic interaction a sharp distinction between habit as the basis of meaning and habit as the basis of belief, between the conditions of possible verification as the structure of meaning and possible verifying instances as the conditions of truth, between meaning as intensional and exemplification as extensional, between the experientially continuous process of meaning development or meaning genesis and the logically continuous generation of schematic possibilities within the internal structure of a meaning as dispositional. Most importantly, it lays the foundation for a strain of radical pluralism that permeates Peirce's philosophy and that will be explored in broader contexts in the following chapters. More immediately, however, the above analysis will be used to explore first Peirce's understanding of the semiotic relation between the ultimate logical interpretant and the dynamical object and then his understanding of what is "given" in the sensing dimension of experience, as these topics relate to the question of his pragmatic pluralism.

HABIT AND THE DYNAMICAL OBJECT

Peirce explicitly relates the problem of meaning to the problem of signs. He claims that the problem of the meaning of intellectual concepts can be solved only by the study of the interpretants, or proper significant effects of signs,[114] and he suggests that the nature of meaning is based upon and understood in terms of the nature of signs.[115] Further, as seen above, Peirce explicitly recognized, late in his career, that his position required an analysis of the internal structure of the concept in a fashion analogous to his analysis of the sign process. As T. L. Short points out, Peirce does not presuppose an unanalyzed notion of meaning but instead explicates meaning in terms of his semiotic.[116] For Peirce, human conduct is itself a cognitive semiotic process. His pragmatic theory of meaning would seem to be part and parcel of his semiotics.

Peirce claimed to have seen for a long time that those concerned with logic must concern themselves with interpretants and ultimately with all sorts of signs. For this reason he thought that "Logic, Considered as Semeiotic," would be an appropriate title for a planned book on logic—a book that was never completed.[117] And, as follows from what was developed earlier, the linkage of semiotic with logic at once links it with mathematics.

It has been seen that in mathematics, and ultimately within the internal structure of all concepts, a series of schemata generated represents alternative possibilities of a predictive rule. Schemata bring to light relationships implicitly operative in rule-guided activity through the interrelationship of predictive or generative rule, activity, and imagery. The difference between the perceptual and the conceptual is not a difference in kind but a difference in the proportions of sensory content and relational structure. All cognition for Peirce involves the perceptual, in the sense that it logically involves an iconic presentation of the cognized object. Thus, as also indicated earlier, in Peirce's pragmatic appropriation of Kantian insights a schema is no longer a product of productive imagination as distinct from the understanding as the faculty of judgment. Rather, both understanding and imagination are unified and transformed into the creative functioning of habit as providing an intensional or semiotic unity between knower and known.[118] The significance of this transformation is well expressed in Klaus Oehler's claim that Peirce forces the function of judgment out of its dominant position, replacing it by the sign function.[119]

As further seen above, meaning for Peirce is indeterminate, in that there is in principle always more to specify. And, its application to the world is indeterminate further, in that its very meaning intends that to which the attribution of a limitless number of nonessential characteristics is always possible. The difference between the concreteness of an existing object and a set of qualities is not the difference between extension and intension. Rather, the intensional meaning contains the meaningfulness of the concreteness of objectivity or "existence" as that which can never be reduced to a set of qualitative aspects or structural relations. This bears directly on the claim that Peirce's argument, which holds that no sign can profess to completely express or represent all the properties of the object of the sign, follows mainly not from a phenomenological analysis of the sign relation but from certain metaphysical assumptions.[120] According to the above analysis this incompleteness is a phenomenological dimension of the awareness of habit as a readiness to respond to more than can ever be specified, a readiness that manifests itself in the ability of the ultimate logical interpretant to generate an indefinite number of schematic forms or logical interpretants representing aspects of an object, each logical interpretant being at once a sign calling forth further logical interpretants.

In making the distinction between the logical interpretant and the ultimate logical interpretant, Peirce holds that logical interpretants are themselves signs that must have logical interpretants, while the ultimate logical interpretant, though it may be a sign in some other way, is not a sign in the same way in which the logical interpretant is a sign.[121] This can be seen in two senses. First, any logical interpretant is a sign that is interpreted by other logical interpretants within the sign system of the concept. The ultimate logical interpretant, as the "self-analyzing" habit, as that concreteness of living habit that generates but can never be exhausted by any number of logical interpretants, is not a sign for any intrasystematic logical interpretant; rather, every such logical interpretant is in a sense a sign of it.[122] Second, a sign stands for its object, not in all respects, but in some respect, while the ultimate logical interpretant, as that which generates the possibility of the grasp of objects in some respect, incorporates the object in its indefinite entirety. Logical interpretants can represent forms or features of objects because the ultimate logical interpretant allows for the grasp of an object as a concrete individual. Interpretants can refer to objects only because we can intend objects as referents.

This focus on objects, however, leads directly to Peirce's recognition of the need "to distinguish the Immediate Object, which is the Object as the Sign itself represents it, and whose Being is thus dependent upon the Representation of it in the Sign, from the Dynamical Object, which is the Reality which by some means contrives to determine the Sign to its Representation."[123] Peirce notes that collateral observation is needed for the dynamical object, and by collateral observation he means previous acquaintance with what the sign denotes.[124] According to Peirce the indexical relation of referring cannot occur unless the mind is already acquainted with thing denoted. Collateral experience of the object is possible because our meanings by their very nature refer to the concreteness of objects having the indeterminateness of an indefinite number of features or aspects. And, past experience of the acquaintance with the dynamical object can lead to the incorporation of more features into the network of logical interpretants potentially available for actualization by the ultimate logical interpretant. For Peirce, the very possibility of "collateral experience requires that a habit has been established in him by which that word calls up a variety of attributes."[125] The establishment of such a habit is the precondition for any judgment, for Peirce holds that "the judgment can never relate to the appearance at the instant of the judgment, because the subject of any judgment must have been known by collateral acquaintance."[126]

This is not a vicious circle but, again, a cumulative process in which the very structure of the ultimate logical interpretant in its relation to logical interpretants allows for the experience of the dynamical object, while acquaintance[127] with the possibilities and constraints of the dynamical object allows for the fuller development of the sign system incorporated within the ultimate logical interpretant.[128] The development of the sign system is an ever-evolving process, but at any moment it has an internal systematic structure unified by the organizing creativity of habit. The systematic structure concerns the sign nature of any meaning qua meaning. The genesis and maintenance of the system concern its relevance to, and workability within, the ongoing context of experience. Thus, ultimate logical interpretants are ultimate in a logical or intrasystematic sense, though subject to change in the ongoing process of successfully organizing experience. In this way habit creates the immediate object under the constraints of the dynamical object that is its ultimate referent, and it provides the vital, living link between signs and the universe.

The ultimate logical interpretant, though the living, developing link between signs and the universe, represents the intrasystematic conceptual unity of any sign system. The final logical interpretant, on the other hand, though an unattainable limit concept representing the static ideal of a habit subject to no further change,[129] nonetheless serves to highlight the dynamics of verification in the maintenance of, or change in, any sign system. This role is well indicated in the characterization of Peirce's final logical interpretant as "that logical interpretant that would survive all possible tests."[130]

It may at first seem surprising that Peirce views abduction in terms of the icon[131] rather than the index. Indexical relations, however, are precisively dependent upon the abductive formation of meanings, on the internal structure of the concept, not the reverse. Until incorporated into a network of logical interpretants under the rule-generated activity of the ultimate logical interpretant, there can emerge in experience no dynamical object as an individual isolatable thing. The dynamical object apart from the structure of meaning is the whole of evolving nature in its indeterminate richness, for apart from our meaning structures, nature as ontologically "there" is, according to Peirce, a continuum that "swims in indeterminacy."[132] In contrast, the dynamical object as the referent of a sign is that which can be singled out from a surrounding environment.[133]

There is a two-way direction operative in which the dynamical object in its metaphysical dimension puts constraints on the ultimate logical interpretant, while the ultimate logical interpretant determines what gives intelligibility to the constraints imposed by the dynamical object in its semiotic relation. The dynamical object is the goal of interpretation, but this goal is possible only through the generation of an interpretant series whose schematic structure is dependent upon the ultimate logical interpretant. And, this interpretive structure will endure only if it serves to objectify the indeterminate richness of reality in workable ways. Here lies the semiotic significance of Peirce's claim that "There is no *thing* which is in itself in the sense of not being relative to the mind, though things which are relative to the mind doubtless *are,* apart from that relation."[134]

Peirce's position here can be illustrated by returning to the function of schemata, this time in relation to immediate interpretants. In addition to distinguishing among the emotional, energetic, and logical interpretants, Peirce distinguishes between the dynamical interpretant, or actual interpretant, and the immediate interpretant.[135] Peirce holds that his "Immediate Interpretant is implied in the fact that each Sign must have its peculiar interpretability before it gets an interpreter."[136] He claims that "The Immediate Interpretant is an abstraction, consisting in a Possibility,"[137] that "the Immediate Interpretant is the schema in her [*sic*] imagination,"[138] and that it is of the nature of an "impression."[139] The Immediate Interpretant as the schema is the possibility of the production of a further aspect of an object within the sign system of the concept, because it is "contained within" the functioning of habit as a rule for its production. In this way "the meaning of a thought is something virtual"; it lies not in what is actually thought.[140] The schema is also the possibility for the production of a further aspect of an object because it incorporates, within its structure, the ponecipuum or "generalized sensation" or sensory core without which nothing in perception could lead to the activation of a particular schema.[141] The being of the schema with its generalized sensation, as the interpretability of a sign within the sign system of the concept, is thus an abstraction from the concreteness of the organizing activities of living habit and from the concreteness of the inexhaustibly rich and varied "sensing" dimension of experience.[142]

Here again it must be remembered that any schema or logical interpretant is also a sign. A logical interpretant, in its function as sign, can call forth a system of further logical interpretants through the organizing force of the ultimate logical interpretant. As a sign, it is constrained in its "peculiar interpretability" by the ultimate logical interpretant, which virtually contains it and legislates its form, and by the so-called impression or sensing dimension of experience which, coming from the side of the dynamical object, becomes absorbed within the initiating stimulus dimension of the schema. Thus, both the ultimate logical interpretant and the dynamical object are responsible for the interpretability of the sign, and this entire relationship is represented in the internal dynamics of meaning as habit. It would seem not only that Peirce explicates meaning in terms of his semiotic, as indicated earlier, but also that he explicates his semiotic in terms of his pragmatic theory of meaning.[143] His pragmatism, theory of meaning, and semiotic are mutually interrelated.[144]

HABIT AND "THE GIVEN"

Habit as the ultimate logical interpretant that constrains the peculiar interpretability of the sign has been discussed in some depth in the earlier part of this chapter. The remainder of the chapter will turn to Peirce's understanding of the sensing dimension of experience, which, as seen above, imposes its own constraints on the interpretability of the sign. And this discussion can best proceed via an analysis of Peirce's understanding of the percipuum as the outcome of the perceptual judgment.

A good deal of attention is beginning to be focused on Peirce's understanding of perceptual judgments and the issue of foundations. Christopher Hookway holds that the percipuum fuses the percept and perceptual judgment into a single whole and represents Peirce's attempt to reject foundationalism, though Hookway never attempts to explicate why this is so.[145] On the other hand, David Gruender, in his discussion of the interrelation of observation and theory in Peirce's philosophy, tends to interpret what is given in the percept along foundationalist lines.[146] Similarly, Jeremiah McCarthy argues that Peirce is led to a foundationalist position because perceptual judgments are immune from doubt.[147] Carl Hausman clearly rejects foundationalist interpretations and recognizes dual meanings of the perceptual judgment in Peirce's philosophy, but he links them to a seemingly univocal meaning of the percipuum.[148] Ultimately, however, the dual nature of the percipuum is central to this issue. The ensuing analysis will attempt to bring into focus Peirce's understanding of the dual senses of the percept, the perceptual judgment, and the percipuum, as well as the role of the ponecept and ponecipuum, in the logic of perceptual awareness, in order to show the radical nature of his rejection of foundationalism. Any discussion of these concepts as used within Peirce's philosophy must be highly extrapolative, but the present way of extrapolating seems well justified by the available texts.[149]

It will be seen that Peirce uses the term *percipuum* in two different senses, a wide sense and a narrow sense, highlighting two corresponding senses of the perceptual judgment.[150] This term seems to have been first used by Peirce in a manuscript of 1903.[151] He there proposes "to consider the percept as it is immediately interpreted in the perceptual judgment, under the name of the 'percipuum.'"[152] Though the term is introduced late in Peirce's career, it can help clarify distinctions toward which he seemed to be groping throughout his writings.

Peirce states that "There is no Percipuum so absolute as not to be subject to possible error."[153] However Peirce is here using the term *percipuum* in its wide sense, a sense that in the preceding context had served the purpose of showing that time is not composed of a series of discrete instants. As he there states, "The percipuum is not an absolute event"; it occurs in a span of time which includes memory and expectation.[154] Here Peirce is concerned with emphasizing the continuity of time or the passing temporal spread in which the percipuum looks to both the past and the future.

What this passage indicates is that when Peirce makes distinctions within the percipuum he is making abstractions for the purpose of analysis. The terms *ponecipuum, percipuum,* and *antecipuum* are used by him to indicate such analytic abstractions.[155] The percipuum in its wide sense, as it actually occurs in the so-called specious present, contains several analytic elements, one of which is the percipuum in its narrow sense. Though the use of these terms may seem representative of the unnecessary obscurity often found in Peirce's writings, they will in fact clarify certain fundamental positions that would be obscured or misinterpreted by the use of more traditional epistemological terms. Thus Hookway points out that the percipuum represents Peirce's attempt to reject "an over simple dichotomy of cognitive processes."[156] Without distinguishing the percipuum in its wide and narrow senses, however, Peirce's radical pragmatic transformation of some traditional epistemic concepts cannot fully come to light.

Peirce's most sustained attempt to distinguish percipuum, antecipuum, and ponecipuum is found in his statement that

> It is a difficult question whether the serial principle permits us to draw sharp lines of demarcation between the percept and the near anticipation, or say the antecept, and between the percept and the recent memory (may I be permitted to call this the ponecept . .), or whether the percept is at once but an extreme case of an antecept and an extreme case of a ponecept. Or rather—I beg the reader's pardon for my awkwardness of statement—the precise-question is not about percept, antecept, and ponecept, but about

> percipuum, antecipuum, and ponecipuum, the direct and uncontrollable interpretations of percept, antecept, and ponecept.[157]

It is with these analytic distinctions and their role in clarifying the nature of the perceptual judgment in its narrow sense that the following pages will be mainly concerned.

A difficulty immediately arises concerning the intended meaning of the above terms. Peirce has labeled the percept as it is immediately interpreted in the perceptual judgment the percipuum. Now, it seems that it is only an interpreted percept that can have near anticipations or predictive meanings adhering to it or, in other words, it is only an interpreted percept that can be an antecept; the antecept is by its very nature interpreted. Thus, what would be an antecipuum, or an interpretation of an antecept? Similarly, it seems that perhaps the ponecept, as a remembered percept, in some way enters into the interpretation of a present percept in the perceptual judgment. What, then, would be an interpretation of a ponecept?

Taking the latter question first, it can be held that a ponecept is an "ingredient in" a ponecipuum. A ponecept, which, as Peirce has clearly indicated, is an abstraction made for purposes of analysis, is a percept as remembered. A synthesis of similar past percepts, or ponecepts, held together as a very primitive "criterion in mind" for the recognition of a present percept, is a ponecipuum. Thus, a ponecipuum, as logically prior to any present percept, is required for the interpretation of the present percept via the perceptual judgment. It provides the synthesized criterion for grasp of presentation as a repeatable content which can activate habit. Indeed, it is the very grasping by the ponecipuum which makes the content repeatable. This ponecipuum is precisely what was seen to be the generalized sensory core of the schematic image within the internal structure of meaning, or in the terminology of Peircean semiotic, what was seen to be the "generalized sensation"[158] that helps constitute the immediate interpretant, providing an ingredient without which nothing in perception could lead to the activation of a particular schema within the structure of the sign system.

The only type of "reference to future experience" implicit in the ponecipuum is the possibility of future presentations of graspable content, which, for purposes of clarity, can perhaps best be termed "possibility of repetition" rather than possibility of future experience. It provides sameness of type[159] but "contains no assertion of a fact."[160] It is that by which one is able to grasp a content that, in becoming a repetition of previous content, can instigate anticipations or "activate" a habit.[161] What instigates activity in the ongoing course of experience is perspectives of objects, appearing facts, but this is possible only because the schematic structure of meaning as habit includes the ponecipuum, or core of generalized sensory content.

The present percept, interpreted in the light of the ponecipuum, is the percipuum in its narrow sense. This percipuum is the outcome of the perceptual judgment in its narrow sense and yields "repeatable content" that serves to activate habit, though, as an analytic stopping point, it provides no anticipation of future experience. The perceptual judgment in its narrow sense is the primitive abductive hypothesis of a present repetition of past experiential content, and the content in fact becomes a repetition of previously experienced contents only as the perceptual judgment does assimilate it to those contents in the abductive process of recognition. Or, as Peirce notes elsewhere, "The percipuum is a recognition of the character of what is past."[162] The percipuum, even in its narrow sense, must "include" the ponecipuum, for it is only in light of the ponecipuum, representing the character of what is past, that the percept can be recognized in the perceptual judgment in its narrow sense. As an analytic stopping point in the analysis of the perceptual judgment in the wide sense, it contains no reference to future experience. As Peirce states, "What two things can be more disparate than a memory and an expectation?"[163] Here it should be reemphasized, however, that while the perceptual judgment in its narrow sense does not include the antecept and antecipuum but instead provides the repetition that gives rise to them with their near anticipations, nevertheless the very character of past assimilation incorporates assimilation of that which has been partially constituted in action. Even the ponecipuum that yields the repetition that activates habit is not the product of a purely passive assimilation. Human creativity and activity enter into every dimension of perceptual awareness.[164]

The antecept can be interpreted as that element of vague, not fully conscious anticipation of future experience that follows upon[165] the perceptual judgment or the recognition of the presented content and that, as explicitly interpreted in the antecipuum, forms the level of full conceptual interpretation or predictive meaning. Furthermore, by his use of terminology—antecept and antecipuum—Peirce indicates quite clearly that the antecept must be seen, for purposes of analysis, as a primitive "layer" in predictive conceptual meaning rather than as an additional "layer" in the recognition of present content. Thus as an analytic stopping point in the analysis of perception one finds a recognized content or percipuum that is totally devoid of reference to future experience yet that, as a recognized content, is dependent upon and is in fact the outcome of a judgment—the perceptual judgment in its narrow sense. Thus, the "sensing dimension," as it enters the structure of human awareness, is not an absolute given but a taken. The content of this analytic stopping place is difficult to signify, for the narrow percipuum in its purity can be expressed neither in the language of objectivity nor in the language of appearing. It is a "First" in that "it cannot be articulately thought," for it loses its "characteristic innocence" in the very attempt.[166] Yet this content is there as an analytic element of the perceptual situation, serving as the basis for our full predictive meanings as developed in the antecept and the antecipuum.

The attempt to explicitly grasp this percipuum yields apprehension of appearance. The focus on appearance is the closest one can come in experience to the grasp of generalized sensory core. But, as seen earlier, even appearances are apprehended as appearances of objectivities and expressed through the language of objectivities because appearances, as generated through the functioning of habit, reflect, in their very emergence, the structurings of objectivities; they reflect the structurings of the very anticipations that one is attempting to withhold in focusing on the appearance qua appearance. The following focus on Peirce's claims can best be understood in terms of the apprehension of appearances as the closest one can come in the ongoing course of experience to the percipuum in its narrow sense as the abstraction of a stopping point in the logical analysis of perception. And here it must be remembered that appearances are not the building blocks of perception but a verification level brought about by a change of focus when a problem arises. What we ordinarily perceive, what instigates action in the ongoing course of experience, are not appearances but appearing objects.

Though Peirce speaks of the percipuum as the percept immediately interpreted in the perceptual judgment, he elsewhere states that "Perhaps I might be permitted to invent the term 'percipuum' to include both percept and perceptual judgment,"[167] since "the differences are so minute and so unimportant logically that it will be convenient to neglect them."[168] As he clarifies his point:

> The forcefulness of the perceptual judgments falls short of the pure unreasonableness of the percept only to this extent, that it does profess to represent the percept, while the perfection of the percept's surdity consists in its not so much as professing anything.[169]

The percept, in its surdity, is infallible because it does not profess anything. And the perceptual judgment is infallible because

> to say that the perceptual judgment is an infallible symptom of the character of the percept means only that in some unaccountable manner we find ourselves impotent to refuse our assent to it in the presence of the percept, and that *there is no appeal from it.*[170]

Thus the percept by itself professes nothing, while the perceptual judgment professes the presence of the percept as a recognized content. Both are infallible, because neither professes the existence of any objective fact or the anticipation of any possibilities of future experience. Future experience cannot show the perceptual judgment in its narrow sense to be in error, since it makes no reference to future experience. Thus Peirce, in replying to the objection that a perceptual judgment is not so utterly beyond all control or check as he says, since it may be revised, states: the "perceptual judgment can only refer to a single percept which can never re-exist; and if I judge that it appears red when it did not appear red, it must, at least be acknowledged that it appeared to appear red."[171]

In distinguishing percept and perceptual judgment, Peirce observes that perceptual judgments are as unlike the percept "as the printed letters in a book, where a Madonna of Murillo is described, are unlike the picture itself."[172] This example may easily lead one to view the relation between percept and perceptual judgment as analogous to the relation between nonlinguistic experience and language. Though Peirce's example is ill chosen, he clearly indicates elsewhere that the perceptual judgment is a higher level in the operation of perception. As he states:

> It may be objected that the terms of the judgment resemble the percept. Let us consider, first, the predicate, "yellow" in the judgment that "this chair appears yellow." This predicate is not the sensation involved in the percept, because it is general. It doesn't even refer particularly to this percept but to a sort of composite photograph of all the yellows that have been. . . . On the whole, it is plain enough that the perceptual judgment is not a copy, icon, or diagram of the percept however rough. It may be reckoned as a higher grade of the operation of perception.[173]

A further clarification of the distinction between the wide and narrow senses of the perceptual judgment can be gained by using as a point of departure Chisholm's claim regarding Peirce's position that "since it takes time to make a perceptual judgment, by the time we have succeeded in judging what it is that direct experience contains, the experience will be past and we will have to appeal to memory."[174] In his analysis, Chisholm makes reference to a statement by Peirce that is perhaps not so clear-cut as at first appears. Peirce writes:

> Now let us take up the perceptual judgment "This wafer looks red." It takes some time to write this sentence, to utter it, or even to think it. It must refer to the state of the percept at the time that it, the judgment, began to be made. But the judgment does not exist until it is completely made. It thus only refers to a memory of the past; and all memory is possibly fallible and subject to criticism and control. The judgment, then, can only mean that so far as the character of the percept can ever be ascertained, it will be ascertained that the waffer looked red.[175]

In just what sense does Peirce mean that memory is subject to criticism and control? As Peirce notes in the paragraph immediately following the quotation above, "Perhaps the matter may be stated less paradoxically."[176] And Peirce proceeds to do this in a discussion that concludes that "to say that a body *is* hard, or red, or heavy, or of a given weight, or has any other property, is to say that it is subject to law and therefore is a statement referring to the future."[177] It is evident that in the above discussion Peirce has switched from the term *looks* to the term *is* and that the character of the percept is ascertained by reference to the future; in this way then, by the test of future experience, memory is subject to criticism and control.

However, in confounding the percipuum in its wide sense and appearing apprehensions, Peirce does make an important point concerning appearances. Though he never explicitly discusses the point, its significance is to be found among the confused statements of the two passages cited above. "All memory is possibly fallible," yet "so far as the character of the percept can never be ascertained, it will be ascertained that the wafer looked red."[178] If one does not continue on to Peirce's "less paradoxical" statements of the issue, this can be taken not as a confused statement concerning future verification but as a statement concerning the nature of the content of the "seeming" statement.

If, as Peirce explicitly states, all memory is fallible, it is difficult to see how that which is indicated by the seeming statement in its attempt to grasp the percipuum in its narrow sense can provide the bedrock of certainty in any absolute sense. The reliability of memory must be questioned not only in regard to what can be predicated from the present content but also in regard to the recognition of the present content itself. Memory is involved in the very recognition of that content which has been seen before and may be seen again, a grasp that allows the content to become the basis for predictive meaning. This basis, then, is not certain but subject to the error of memory and incapable of providing an indubitable bedrock of empirical knowledge in any foundationalist sense of the terms.

What is provided is not the absolute certainty of foundationalist claims but "pragmatic certainty." The apprehension of an appearance is indubitable, in the sense that its falsity is inconceivable. It is beyond conceivable doubt, because to doubt it in the sense that one thinks it may be proven wrong is senseless; indeed, it is literally so. To doubt it is to put into question something for which there is no tool for getting "behind" it to compare it with anything more fundamental. For us, it must itself be the final court of appeal. The apprehension of an appearance is not certainly true as opposed to possibly false. It is "certain" in the sense that neither truth nor falsity is applicable to it. The perceptual judgment in its narrow sense cannot even be labeled "certainly correct" as opposed to "possibly incorrect." There is no correct or incorrect recognition involved at this level, for what the percipuum is is determined only in its recognition and can be determined in no other way. It becomes a "repetition" of previous contents only by being assimilated to those contents in the perceptual judgment. In relation to more traditional views, this conclusion is surely more paradoxical than the conclusion that the perceptual judgment, in its wide sense, is fallible because it can be proven wrong by reference to future experience. Perhaps the novelty of the former conclusion, coupled with his own failure to clarify the conceptual distinctions toward which he was groping, led Peirce subtly to switch in his attempt to make his position seem "less paradoxical." However, apart from such speculation, it does seem that Peirce's confused discussion stems from a careless slipping back and forth between two concepts that he later clearly though briefly distinguished.

Peirce's use of the perceptual judgment in its narrow sense has been discussed in detail because it is the "more paradoxical" and less emphasized of the two senses. That this is so is no doubt due both to Peirce's brief and late exposition of a distinction in levels of judgment and to the preconceived assumption that what is the outcome of a judgment must be capable of being shown to be true or false. Bernstein points out that if the perceptual judgment cannot be true or false it is not a judgment[179] and, again, that if there is a hypothetical element involved in every perceptual judgment, then every perceptual judgment is fallible and subject to future tests.[180] Conversely, it is McCarthy's acceptance of the claim that perceptual judgments are immune from doubt that allows him to hold that Peirce makes use of an observation-theory distinction that turns him into a foundationalist.[181] The perceptual judgments in their narrow senses do have a "hypothetical element,"[182] for the judgment is a hypothesis that a content is "the same as" that which has been seen before or "appears as."[183] However, the above analysis has shown that these narrow uses of the perceptual judgment are not fallible and subject to future tests, for they make no references to future experience. As Peirce states, their surdity is almost complete. They cannot be characterized as true or false, for, as indicated above, we have no more fundamental perceptual tool by which to assert their truth or falsity. To deny the term *judgment* to that which can be characterized as neither true nor false is one way to avoid the frequent confusions that pervade Peirce's analysis of perception because of his dual uses of this term, and it allows one to follow a more conventional terminological procedure. It is not, however, to offer an objection to that concept that Peirce intends by the term.[184] By characterizing this primitive synthesis in terms of a perceptual judgment which yet cannot be true or false, he brings home more forcefully the radical novelty of his rejection of both foundationalism and anti-foundationalism. What is "given" at the most fundamental level of perceptual awareness is in fact a "taken," and it incorporates both the nature of the taking and the nature of what is taken. Here it should be noted that Peirce's use of the perceptual judgment in its narrow sense is not, as it may at first seem, a narrowly confined part of his philosophy. For the fact that even at this level what is grasped is a product of the synthesizing activity of mind has already been seen to be an important factor in understanding the sensuous core of the schematic image in the internal structure of meaning as dispositional. Moreover, the importance of the perceptual judgment in its narrow sense will further be seen in chapter 5, where it will have a crucial bearing both on Peirce's transitional move from epistemic interests to more cosmic concerns and on the content of his metaphysical claims.

The perceptual judgment in its wide sense is indubitable, not in the sense that the discovery of its falsity is inconceivable, for its truth or falsity may be ascertained by future experience, but in the sense that there are no positive grounds to stimulate doubt present in the perceptual situation. As Peirce has stressed in his rejection of Descartes' universal doubt, we cannot feign doubt.[185] Unless some positive ground for doubt is given in the perceptual situation, perceptual judgments and certain vague beliefs[186] must be taken as indubitable, for they cannot seriously be doubted—though they are eminently fallible, since subject to the test of future experience. Thus, we arrive in a broad sense at Peirce's "fallibilism." The fallibility of the perceptual judgment in its wide sense, as it actually occurs in the passage of the present and makes a claim about an objective state of affairs, lies in the fact that it will be rejected as false if it does not fit into the general interpretive context as discussed earlier. The indubitability at this level enters in the sense that the formation of the perceptual judgment cannot be controlled and is beyond logical criticism in its formation. While we cannot critically control the judgment, however, we can criticize its results and conclude, based on future experience, that it is false. However, underlying the very possibility of these commonsense indubitables which may turn out to be false is an indubitability to which neither truth nor falsity is applicable, one that is "pragmatically certain." David Savan aptly characterizes this type of distinction when he notes the difference between indubitables that cannot conceivably be doubted and indubitables that are so only because there is no positive ground to stimulate doubt.[187]

This chapter has attempted to show the way in which, for Peirce, perceptual facts at their very core emerge neither from mind alone nor from the dynamic reality of the universe alone but from the interaction of the two that constitutes experience. This way involves the analytic certitudes that determine what types of facts conceivable may be, as well as the pragmatic certitudes of what is "given" in experience. And it is the interrelation of these two types of certitudes that reveals the radical nature of the inherent pluralism involved in the grasp of perceptual facts. For the analytic certitudes of alternative conceptual networks that delineate facts enter into the very appearances that serve as the indubitables in the verification process. Since the habits constitutive of conceptual networks have their own schematic sets, each schema having its own sensuous core, any content grasped would be assimilated, if at all possible, to the ponecipuum included in one of the schemata implied by the habit. The interpretive concept and its verification instances at all of its levels must justify themselves by their workability as a unity in the ongoing course of experience. In the very restructuring or reinterpreting of facts when expectations are frustrated, there is a restructuring of the appearance, for appearances in their very emergence reflect the structurings of objectivities.

Even the sensuous core of the objectivity, which the focus on appearance attempts to approach, is not a brute given; rather, it is partially constituted through its interpretive assimilation, via the ponecipuum, to past experience. Only within the context of these interacting features shot through with interpretive dimensions yielding alternative possible structurings at all levels can a dynamical object be brought forth as an individual, isolatable thing. But, as has been stressed, throughout all these levels, the brute "thereness" of the whole of evolving nature as the dynamical object pressures our interpretations in some directions rather than others and limits the range of possible interpretations in terms of workability. Within this interactive context of interpretation and constraint, different structurings yield different isolatable dynamical objects. Just as "Thirdness pours in on us through every avenue of sense,"[188] so pluralism follows in its wake.

At this point one may object that this entire chapter has based too many conclusions on an extrapolation of Peirce's understanding of the internal structure of meaning as habit. However, if doing so has thrown any light on Peirce's position, it would seem justified in accordance with his own method, as stated in the context of his semiotic, of developing his position by reasoning "what sort of thing *ought* to be noticeable and *then* searching for its appearance."[189] From the backdrop of the light that hopefully has been cast by the features of Peirce's understanding of meaning as habit as developed above, the next chapter can turn to the potential significance of his proofs of realism for the issue of pragmatic pluralism.

CHAPTER 3

Habit, Temporality, and Peirce's Proofs of Realism

It is a not uncommon objection to Peirce's pragmatism that his pragmatic theory of meaning makes it impossible to meaningfully assert the existence of the real potentiality upon which he insists. Yet Peirce not only insists upon the reality of causal laws or genuine potentialities but stresses that the pragmatist qua pragmatist must embrace realism as opposed to nominalism. The crucial significance of this objection to Peirce's acceptance of realism as opposed to nominalism is aptly captured in the simple observation by Arthur Burks that his pragmatic theory of meaning is incompatible with his metaphysics.[1] In short, there is a contradiction running throughout his philosophic thought. As Peter Turley has forcefully stated the objection, realism, like his nominalism, "is unverifiable speculation, therefore meaningless from the standpoint of Peirce's pragmatism."[2] The questionableness of Peirce's assertion of the reality of lawfulness within the context of a pragmatic philosophy can be more fully clarified by the following somewhat detailed objection:

> The summary view of lawfulness (nominalistic) and the counterfactual view (realistic), give rise to exactly the same set of experiential consequences; indeed, the only difference between them is not what happens but rather what does not but would or could have happened, and so it is not a matter of experience; consequently, there is no real difference between the two theories, and the dispute is eliminated by the pragmatic criterion.[3]

More prominent in the literature than concern with the meaningfulness of Peirce's realism are the attempts to justify Peirce's "proofs" of realism. The ensuing discussion will deal with both of these issues, not in turn, but together, as they are inseparably interrelated and mutually clarifying. Further, it will show that the way in which these issues mutually clarify each other points toward the inherent pluralism involved in the very emergence of lawfulness within experience.

Peter Skagestad presents a forceful defense of Peirce's pragmatic realism as an explanation of "why the scientific manipulation of language affects our interaction with the world in the way in which it does." He argues that for Peirce such a claim is susceptible to the cumulative effect of inductive confirmation or disconfirmation. Though the nonfulfillment of an inductive prediction does not overthrow realism, the nonfulfillment of all inductive predictions would overthrow it; hence, each nonfulfillment of an inductive prediction counts as evidence against it, while each fulfillment counts as evidence in its favor. Pragmatic realism is thus an empirical hypothesis about science. That there is such a thing as science supplies empirical support for the claims of realism.[4] In a somewhat different but related vein, Susan Haack argues that Peirce's realism is best conceived as a "kind of high-level abductive hypothesis"[5] needed to account for the possibility of there being genuine science, thus receiving indirect verification.[6]

The development of these arguments contains important insights into the compatibility of Peirce's pragmatic verificationism and his realism. By focusing on the level of science and/or scientific language, however, the full strength of such insights is not utilized, for realism as an inductively supportable and supported hypothesis begins, for Peirce, neither at the level of language nor at the level of science, but at the level of rudimentary perceptual experience. Realism is incorporated in language because the structure of language incorporates the meaningful structure of rudimentary perceptual experience;[7] science incorporates realism because the structure of scientific prediction reflects the structure of such experience.[8] And, since perceptual experience, at its most fundamental level, will be seen to be rooted in the primitive experience of temporality,[9] it is in the experience of temporality that the basis for both the meaningfulness and the cumulative verification of realism will be found. Further, rooting the issues in this fundamental level will be seen to resolve the supposed contradictory claims that are held to be "undeniably there" in Peirce's defense of realism.[10] The following discussion will first turn to the need for a focus on this more fundamental level.

Peirce, in discussing the real lawfulness of nature, notes the manner in which the scientist grasps the potential through the actual when he observes that "what would be, can, it is true, only be learned through observation of what happens to be."[11] What this seems to indicate is that the particular content of any particular law can be ascertained only by reference to actual occurrences. After a certain number of experiments in which a series of actual events takes place, the scientist has discovered the content of a law and exemplifies his extra knowledge by prediction. In brief, we establish what would be by what is and, in turn, verify what would be by what is. The issue at hand, however, is not merely the question of how one establishes the particular content of a particular law but the very meaningfulness of the assertion that the potentialities of lawfulness are something real over and above the actual instances that we interpret as their exemplifications. And, if any law has content only by reference to the actual, what can we even mean by the assertion of the reality of potentiality as something distinguishable from the actual? Although scientific experimentation tends to provide a cumulative confirmation of a predictable uniformity in nature, the nature of this uniformity still remains at issue.[12]

The attempt has also been made to defend Peirce's pragmatic realism from the direction of logic, but this again begs the very issue in question. Such a defense[13] focuses on Peirce's claim that his pragmatism is concerned with the consequence as a relation between an antecedent and a consequent rather than with the consequent itself. However, a close examination of Peirce's definition of a consequence as a relation between an antecedent and a consequent shows that it does not provide an answer to the problem but requires a previous solution before it can itself be interpreted. Peirce defines the consequence in the following passage:

> Scotus and the later scholastics usually dealt not with the syllogism but with an inferential form called a consequence. The consequence has only one expressed premise, called an antecedent; and its conclusion is called the consequent; and the proposition which asserts that in case the antecedent be true, the consequent is true, is called the consequence.[14]

Thus, by a "consequence" Peirce means a conditional proposition or an implication relation. However, precisely what is at issue is the nature of this implication relation. Does it mean that when A happens, B will happen, or does it mean that if A had happened, B would have happened, although A has not and will not, in fact, happen? This is the crux of the logical issue between realism and nominalism,[15] and an appeal to the consequence in support of realism merely begs the issue of the nature of the consequence.

The answer to the above problem begins to emerge neither at the level of the sophisticated elaboration of logical relationships nor at the level of sophisticated scientific experimentation and prediction, but at the more fundamental level of the epistemic foundations for such endeavors. And such a foundation must provide an answer for the question: How can any experience of what is actual provide a meaningful content for the concept of unactualized possibilities, of a reality that by its very nature is more than the sum of all actualities? That relations of qualitative events are given in perception rather than discrete atomic qualitative appearances will not by itself handle the problem at its most fundamental level, for whatever is given is actual. Even if actual relationships are given, how do we get from this to a claim concerning the unrealized potentialities of real relations? The direction to be followed here is indicated in a general way by Murphey when he notes that Peirce required a "property characterizing unactualized possibilities which would be itself actual so that it could be observed. . . . Peirce found such a property in continuity."[16] Thus Peirce emphasizes, concerning continuity, that "points are nothing but possibilities, until they are actually marked. Therefore, those intermediate points, being possible, are already there in the only sense there is in speaking of unmarked points."[17]

Here again, however, the answer cannot be found in terms of an abstract concept of continuity. Rather, the abstract elaboration of continuity for Peirce gains its fullness of meaning from the concreteness of experience. As Peirce cautions, "it may be held that we can be justified in inferring true generality, true continuity. But I do not see in what way we ever can be justified in doing so unless we admit the cotary propositions, and in particular, that such continuity is given in perception; that is . . . we seem to perceive a genuine flow of time."[18] Thus, the claim for true continuity or true generality[19] is rooted ultimately in the experience of a durational present. And it will be seen that the concrete meaning of unactualized possibilities, of genuine alternatives and genuine potentialities, is gained by reference to the experiential awareness within the durational present of habit as a rule of organization of unlimited possibilities and as a readiness to respond to more than can ever be specified or actualized. The meaningfulness of the content of Peirce's assertion that predictive regularity is to be understood in terms of the potentialities of real causal relationships is gained by a sophisticated elaboration of or abstraction from the reference to the primitive experience of unactualized possibilities or real potentialities as this occurs through the functioning of habit in the flow of time. It has been noted that "It is the lawlike character of our experience which accounts for the meaning of our concepts and propositions; for it is the lawlike character of our experience which accounts for the properties, a description of which constitutes meaning."[20] However, it will be seen that though it is the lawlike or uniform character of our experience that accounts for the possibility of our meanings, it is the structure of our meanings that accounts for the understanding of such a lawlike character as the exemplification of real potentialities, of real generals.

This understanding of the role of habit as yielding an experience of unactualized possibilities is implicit in the previous development of meaning as habit, for a habit is a "would-be," and "no agglomeration of actual happenings can ever completely fill up the meaning of a 'would-be.'"[21] There it was seen that the significance of the content of the logical interpretant lies in the way in which it comes into being; such an explicit structure represents an aspect of the dispositional structural order by which it is regulated. Just as a continuum may generate an unlimited number of cuts within itself, so a disposition as a rule of organization contains within itself an unlimited number of possibilities of specific aspects of structure to be generated. And, just as with the continuum, one may elicit any particular cut, but cannot exhaust via enumeration all possible cuts, so one can elicit any particular set of appearances and acts desired, but cannot exhaust via enumeration all possibilities.

Further, in none of these cases is the inability to exhaust via enumeration all possibilities a contingent fact; it is intrinsic to the nature of the generating rule. As Peirce states, "A true continuum is something whose possibilities of determination no multitude of individuals can exhaust," while "a habit or general idea is a living feeling, infinitesimal in duration and immediately present, but still embracing innumerable parts."[22] And, continues Peirce, in such an "absence of boundedness a vague possibility of more than is present is directly felt."[23] Such a sense of vague possibility includes the sense of efficacy, for "feeling which has not yet emerged into immediate consciousness is already affectible and already affected. In fact, this is habit, by virtue of which an idea is brought up into present consciousness by a bond that had already been established between it and another idea while . . . it was still in futuro."[24] Peirce summarizes the import of the above: "In the presence of this continuity of feeling, nominalistic maxims appear futile."[25]

Skagestad's recognition that the beginning of Peirce's pragmatic arguments for realism is found in directing us "towards something different from practical facts, namely to general ideas, as the true interpreters of our thought,"[26] is indeed significant. However, its significance is found in the fact that at the very basis of general ideas is not just predictability according to "a general description, namely the experimenter's plan or purpose,"[27] but a rudimentary, concrete, lived through experience of the generative potentialities constitutive of real lawfulness.[28] Thompson has argued convincingly that "Scholastic realism is 'too nominalistic' for Peirce because it remains compatible with construing a true generalization as a conjunction of true singular statements." Rather, for Peirce, individuals are understood as instances of the generalization.[29] For Peirce, realism must be understood in this way, for the potentialities of real lawfulness are immediately felt in the functioning of habit as the generative, structuring rule for the production of perceived objectivities. The meaning of potentiality or the would-be is to be found in the general purposiveness inherent in the felt actuality of habit as that which can never be exhausted in its results. The felt functioning of meaning as dispositional, then, is the source not only of our sense of the concrete unity of objectivity as more than a collection of appearances, but also of our sense of a reality whose possibilities of being experienced transcend all actual experiences. Indeed, "a pragmatist must subscribe to the doctrine of real possibility because nothing other than this can be so much as meant by saying an object possesses a character."[30]

Thus, the conceiving mind cannot, by the very nature of meaning, be tied down to a consciousness that apprehends actualities only, for the implicit content of our concepts includes meaningful assertions about potentialities that reach out beyond that which will ever be actualized. Embodied in the actuality of our conceptual structures as dispositional, then, is a sense of reality that transcends actual occasions of experience. Such a sense is rooted directly in a recognition of time as process, for in the process of lived time is to be found the basis for the primitive epistemological "feel" of continuity, of the functioning of meaning as dispositional, and, within it, the primitive epistemological "feel" of real potentialities or real dynamic tendencies. As Peirce stresses, "There is no span of present time so short as not to contain . . . something for the confirmation of which we are waiting."[31] But this "peculiar element of the present, that it confronts us with ideas which it forces upon us . . . is something which accumulates in wholes of time and dissipates the more minutely the course of time is scrutinized."[32]

The very structure of meaning is grounded in a primordial experience of time as process. What occurs within the present awareness is not the apprehension of a discrete datum in a moment of time, but the time-extended experiential "feel" within the passing present of a readiness to respond to more than can ever be specified. Thus Peirce points out that "if we wish to know what the percipuum of the course of time is, all we have to do is abstain from sophisticating it, and it will be plain enough . . ."[33] It has been argued that Peirce meant not to literally attack the question of realism experimentally but to show, against Hume, that the claims of realism "make sense, or at least better sense than their alternatives." In short, "Peirce found his approach to be more sane, more reasonable, and more in accord with 'our scheme of the universe.'"[34] According to the present interpretation of Peirce's proofs, he would hold his position to be more in accord with "our scheme of the universe" because it is the view that is sensible, but literally so.

One may, if one wishes, ignore this percipuum of the course of time and insist on interpreting time as a series of knife-edged moments, and, along with this, one may insist that predictability is nothing but the regularity of such moments, decrying the meaninglessness of the assertion of any supposed causal relatedness or genuine potentiality or real generality. Indeed, in taking away the durational present, in reducing the process of lived time to a series of knife-edged moments, one has taken away the basis for the primitive epistemological "feel" of continuity. And, in so doing, one has ruled out of court the very possibility of the functioning of meaning as a generative rule and hence has ruled out of court the basis for a primitive epistemic "feel" of real potentialities structuring the very character of emerging actualities. But, in removing this temporal basis of felt continuity, in removing the primitive experiential sense of the reality of unactualized potentialities, one has taken away the very possibilities of perceiving a world of physical objectivities. Peirce well warns about this, pointing out that "So long as we trust to common sense, the properties of a true continuum are a matter of course," while through our abstract elaborations "we founder from quagmire into quicksand."[35]

The significance of this relation between the "sense" of realism, temporality, and the perceived world in resolving supposed contradictions in Peirce's "proofs" of realism will be the focus of the ensuing discussion. There are two major areas to be explored: first, the possible inconsistency, or, at best, ambiguity of purpose, in Peirce's "experimental proof of realism," as it is generally called; second, the possible inconsistency of this proof with his supposed "a priori proof" for realism.

Peirce, in performing an experiment to provide evidence for his realism, drops a stone to the floor. He then concludes:

> A thousand other such inductive predictions are getting verified every day, and one would have to suppose every one of them to be merely fortuitous in order reasonably to escape the conclusion that general principles are really operative in nature. This is the doctrine of scholastic realism.[36]

Thompson, focusing on Peirce's experimental proof, poses the dichotomy of rhetorical illustration of commonsense belief versus experimental testing of a dubitable hypothesis,[37] and as Skagestad well summarizes, he argues that "Peirce wants to do more than the former and does not succeed in doing the latter."[38] Skagestad's own claim is that Peirce is in fact offering experimental testing. The experimental evidence for realism is not just the fall of the stone but the fact that everybody predicts that the stone will fall and that it actually does fall. If it had failed to fall, this would have counted as evidence against realism.[39] Once again, the present work agrees with Skagestad's position but finds that it does not go far enough in its defense of Peirce because it takes the language of science as its starting point. But, to further develop this point, it will be necessary to first explore Peirce's supposed "a priori" proof of realism, his argument for the inconceivability of a chance world. Here Skagestad, like other critics of Peirce, does find an inconsistency between it and the experimental "proof." Skagestad, adhering to "the principle of charity," locates this "unavoidable inconsistency" near the periphery of Peirce's thought. However, such charitableness may not be necessary in this instance. The following discussion will attempt to show that Peirce's supposed a prior proof for realism, far from being incompatible with his experimental proof, provides an illuminating pathway to it.

Peirce's discussion of the inconceivability of a chance world emerges within the context of his discussion of clerical arguments for the existence of God.[40] The purpose of his general discussion is to show not that the orderliness we find in our experience proves the reality of Thirdness but that such orderliness cannot prove the existence of God. Peirce argues that both a chance universe and an orderly universe would allow for our world as we experience it, because the uniformities necessary for predictability, which constitute our orderly world, emerge as uniformities in relation to an organizing, delineating mind.[41] A universe of chance or a universe of order, not related to human intents is, according to Peirce, equally abundant in possibilities of order for mind to discriminate.[42] From this concretely rich universe, through the perspective of a meaning system rooted in active interest and intent, meaningful uniformities emerge within our world.[43] As has already been seen from a different perspective, facts or objects emerge neither from mind alone nor from the universe alone but from the interaction of the two that constitutes experience. And predictable order is always among facts.

Thus, experience of a chance world is inconceivable, not because it is a priori impossible, but because of the way intelligence operates. Indeed, an intelligent organism, set down in any chaos, would proceed to elicit order necessary for its ongoing activities.[44] Because of this Peirce concludes that the only way the uniformities of our experienced world could prove the existence of God were if the existence of finite minds proved the existence of Infinite Mind.[45] For Peirce, the interesting issue is not whether the universe, apart from an interested mind, is one of order or chance but what experience would be like if there were no possible uniformities interesting for human activities.[46] And his conclusion here is most instructive. If this latter were to be the case, there would be no perception of objectivities at all. Experience of a chance world would be the experience of a mind that refused to organize, or, in other terms, "A world of chance is simply our actual world viewed from the standpoint of an animal at the vanishing point of intelligence." There would be neither memory nor expectation.[47] Memory, for Peirce, like expectation, "depends on a law of organization" rooted in dispositionally generated activity, founded ultimately in the nature of temporality. Thus, Peirce claims that "The world of memory is the world of time,"[48] but "were the instants independently actual, as they are in the Time of the analysts, memory would be a perpetual miracle."[49] The existence of memory is itself, for Peirce, a proof for continuity, for "if it were not so, nobody could have any memory."[50]

A world without order, then, would be a world without recognizable things. That the universe contains possibilities or order relevant to human activities is shown by the very existence, within experience, of a perceptual world of objectivities. That this uniformity, which allows for our perceived world, is grasped in terms of Thirdness or real dynamic potentialities is shown, not by the inconceivability of a world without order or uniformity, but by an examination of the nature of the perceptual experience within which our orderly world emerges. Such an examination reveals that these uniformities are experienced, in rudimentary perceptual awareness, not as regularities among discrete characters occurring in discrete moments but as the product of creative, dynamic tendencies that are immediately felt in the temporal flow of the durational present. In short, that we have a perceptual world is evidence of the availability within the universe of abstractable uniformities interesting to us, whatever be their nature apart from us. An examination of the perceptual experience in which the experience of these uniformities is rooted uncovers the basis for the meaningfulness of realism as the explanation of the nature of the uniformities. The claim that there are ontologically real causal forces operative in the universe that creatively structure emerging facts gains its explanatory meaningfulness in the concreteness of experience, for such dynamic creativity is immediately felt in the functioning of habit through the passage of time. This meaningful claim, which is, if not willfully ignored, implicit in the very heart of the conceiving mind, is then inductively verified by the continual availability of our perceptual world and by the prediction of science.

But this statement brings the discussion back to the experimental proof for realism. And, by now, the full significance of the defense of Peirce in terms not just of the fall of the stone but the fulfilled expectation of the fall of the stone[51] can begin to emerge, for it can be seen that there is no dichotomy, such as that posed above by Thompson, between "rhetorical illustration of commonsense belief and experimental testing of a dubitable hypothesis." What is being verified by experimental testing is, ultimately, not a particular scientific law or scientific laws in general, but the commonsense expectation of predictive reliability rooted in the primitive epistemic "feel" of real potentiality. What is being verified is a belief that is dubitable in principle—and that is, in fact, often doubted at the abstract, reflective levels of science, logic, and philosophy—but that, at the level of rudimentary perceptual experience, is so fundamental to our very sense of our world, and is so well verified by the continual availability of our perceptual world, that its illustration in verifying instances does, indeed, seem rhetorical. As Peirce points out, a baby makes "acquaintance with the flow of causation. Acquaintance with the flow of causation so early as to make it familiar before speech."[52]

If all predictive reliability were lost, we should, as Skagestad indicated, no longer have science,[53] but then neither should we have a perceptual world. However, that we should have pragmatic evidence for the falsity of realism[54] is for Peirce not the case. For, to no longer have our perceptual world is to have given up the organizing activity of mind and, with it, the sense of dispositionally organized felt possibilities, memory, and expectation. And that same temporally rooted, dispositionally organized sense of expectation, which is at the heart of the sense of realism and the sense of a perceive world, is at the heart, also, of the very possibility of pragmatic evidence. As Peirce states, concerning the same temporally rooted percipuum that makes nominalistic maxims futile, "it is remarkable that in case we do not accept the percipuum's own account of itself . . . then it would seem that there is nothing that empirical truth can mean except accordance with what is given in those instants, which in this case, in no way testify concerning one another or in any way refer to one another."[55] Ultimately, then, for Peirce, to deny the sense of realism embedded in perceptual awareness is to deny the possibility of truth in terms of verification, both at the level of science and at the level of common sense. Thus, the primordial experience of temporal flow at the heart of perceptual awareness is foundational both for the sense of realism and for the very possibility of its experimental proof. Because of Peirce's pragmatic understanding of meaning as habit and its experiential dimensions, the claim of realism is meaningful and necessarily embedded in our commonsense perception of the world, and it is this meaningful claim that is being empirically verified through fulfilled prediction. Several important implications for Peirce's general position lie implicit in the above development.

First, the very way in which Peirce's proofs for realism involve the ordering discriminations of intelligence points toward the possibility of an inherent pluralism implicit in his arguments, for what laws one finds are partially dependent on the creative discriminations one brings, and alternative ways of discriminating may lead to alternative law-governed uniformities within experience.

Second, it should not be surprising, in retrospect, that Peirce's experimental proof of realism leads to the very roots of lived experience, since experience for Peirce is inherently experimental, embodying the dynamics of scientific method as the lived experimental activity of the scientist. Scientific method involves a noetic creativity that organizes experience and directs our activity, a creativity whose adequacy is tested in the ongoing course of experience. For Peirce, scientific method is the only method of fixing belief, for it is the only method by which beliefs must be tested and corrected by what experience presents. Further, as the previous chapter well illustrated, the creative abductions of science that provide an organizational focus for directed activity shade into everyday "perceptual judgments without any sharp line of demarcation between them."[56] Peirce's concern with scientific method is with the dynamics of experimental activity, not with the reification of its contents, and this experimental activity is embedded, according to him, in the most rudimentary experiential dynamics that give rise to the perceived world. This pervasiveness of experimental method will prove significant most immediately for interpreting his derivation of the categories in the next chapter.

Finally, there are key metaphysical implications involved in Peirce's understanding of the sense of realism that pervades experience. The sense of realism has been seen to be inseparable from the functioning of habit in the flow of time, for a disposition or habit as a rule of generation is something whose possibilities of determination no multitude of actually generated instances can exhaust. Peirce's dispositional theory of meaning leads to a metaphysics of realism as opposed to nominalism, not a realism of eternal essences, but a "process realism" in which there are real modes of behavior that govern what occurs. Laws, which outrun any number of actualities, are, as modes of behavior, the source of the structures emerging in what occurs. Human habits of response are precisely lawful modes of behavior structuring emerging activities. Thus Peirce states of the pragmatist, "That he will have no difficulty with Thirdness is clear enough because he will hold that conformity of action to general intentions is as much given in perception as is the element of action itself, which cannot really be mentally torn away from such general purposiveness."[57] The concrete functioning of habit provides, epistemically, the conceptual counterpart of the real lawfulness held to exist in the world, and it provides, ontologically, an example of this real lawfulness.[58]

The awareness of habit as a disposition or readiness to respond to more than can be specified gives a concrete meaning to the concept of a 'process realism,' of a real lawfulness that outruns and governs unactualized possibilities. Further, the sense of process realism at once would seem to provide, for Peirce, an experiential basis for the rejection of deterministic hypotheses, one not presented in "The Doctrine of Necessity Examined."[59] For the sense of unactualized possibilities embedded in meaning as dispositional brings a sense of real alternatives into the very heart of perceptual awareness, providing an experientially meaningful basis for the rejection of deterministic hypotheses, a directly felt sense of possibilities and of the spontaneity of choice among them. To hold that this "sense of realism," which is inherent both in our everyday perception of the world around us and in the assertions of science, is indeed metaphysically veridical involves showing, ultimately, that for Peirce, the features of experience revealed through his pragmatic examination of experience are at once the features of the ontologically real.[60] This, like the pervasiveness of experimental method, will be the topic of the following chapter.

That Peirce does intend an intimate interrelation between his pragmatic analyses of experience and his metaphysics is to be found in his claim that

> Suffice it to say once more that pragmatism is, in itself, no doctrine of metaphysics, no attempt to determine any truth of things. It is merely a method of ascertaining the meanings of hard words

> and of abstract concepts. All pragmatists of whatever stripe will cordially assent to that statement. *As to the ulterior and indirect effects of practicing the pragmatic method, that is quite another affair.*[61]

Such effects are detailed elsewhere:

> There are certain questions commonly reckoned as metaphysical, and which certainly are so, if by metaphysics we mean ontology, which as soon as pragmatism is once sincerely accepted, cannot logically resist settlement. These are for example, What is reality? Are necessity and contingency real modes of being? Are the laws of nature real? Can they be assumed to be immutable or are they presumably results of evolution? Is there any real chance or departure from real law?[62]

Or, as he succinctly summarizes, "Pragmatism . . . is the forerunner of a new metaphysical light."[63] And, from the backdrop of this chapter, it can be anticipated that Peirce's synechism, rooted ultimately in temporality, will be central to its focus. This anticipation stands in radical opposition to the view that is well represented in the recent claim that Peirce's synechism "incorporated his strong pragmatic position on the relative demerit of metaphysics" and is, in fact, not a metaphysical doctrine but solely a regulative principle of logic.[64] Peirce's pragmatism is far from being an antimetaphysical tool for clarifying the meaning of terms. Rather, the very tool leads to a particular ontological content. Such a content belongs both to ontology and "to 'epistemology,' an atrocious translation of Erkenntnislehre."[65] A further development of this "mutual belonging" leads directly to the topic of Peirce's phenomenology or phaneroscopy and the derivation of the categories.

CHAPTER 4

Pragmatic Experimentalism and the Derivation of the Categories

It is generally held that Peirce's philosophy incorporates diverse methods for obtaining the categories: a priori deduction from mathematical principles and phenomenological inquiry. This diversity is in turn held to evince different systems chronologically developed[1] or a conflict between naturalist and transcendentalist strains of his thought.[2] The present chapter will first attempt to show that one method, the phenomenological method, is at work in Peirce's derivation of the categories, though he of course did not use this term until late in his career, and to decipher the distinctively pragmatic character of its dynamics with the implicit pluralism it involves. The remainder of the chapter will then examine the significance of this view of Peirce's phenomenology for interpreting his understanding of the nature of the metaphysical enterprise and the dynamics of its relation to his phenomenology.

The phenomenology Peirce develops could be called "hermeneutical phenomenology," but perhaps, in the context of his pragmatism, "experimental phenomenology" is a more appropriate label, one that points more directly to its key pragmatic features. Peirce's categories of Firstness, Secondness, and Thirdness will be seen to be an interrelated set of meanings, abductively generated as a tool for focusing on the richness of experience in order to elicit its illusive, "intangible"[3] but pervasive textures, "traits,"[4] "tones or tints."[5] And, as with all sets of meanings, it is necessary to distinguish their abductive, creative genesis within experience, the logical priority of these abductively generated meanings for the future delineation of experience, and the verification of the adequacy of their application in the ongoing course of experience.

These experimental dynamics can best be brought to light by first examining in just what sense Peirce's phenomenology "simply scrutinizes the direct appearances" or confines itself to "honest, single-minded observation of the appearances."[6] It involves "pure observation," in the sense that it does not make judgments concerning the reality of what is observed. As he states, "Phaneroscopy is the description of the phaneron; and by the phaneron I mean the collective total of all that is in any way or in any sense present to the mind, quite regardless of whether it corresponds to any real thing or not."[7] In this sense, it is concerned with phenomena in their dimension of Firstness.[8] When Peirce claims that his phenomenological derivation of the categories is an experiential derivation, he is "taking experience in its broadest sense"[9] and to include not only experience of the real world but experience of ideal worlds, illusion, and so on.[10] In brief, as Peirce states, "In high philosophy experience is the entire cognitive result of living, and illusion is, for its purposes, just as much experience as is real perception";[11] it "includes interpretations quite as truly as it does the matter of sense."[12] Thus experience in the context of Peirce's phenomenology cannot be understood in the more restricted Piercean sense in which "the world of experience" is equated with "the world of fact."[13] Phenomenology involves pure observation, then, in that it observes the entire range of experience, possible and actual, without judgments of objectivity.

Phenomenology is further concerned with the observation of appearances in that it does not impose upon the experiences the frameworks of any of the sciences. Thus Peirce points out that though the psychologist and the astronomer look upon the same world as the phenomenologist, what they observe is different.[14] It is in this sense that one needs the ability to see what presents itself, just as it is. As Peirce stresses, one needs the "observational powers of the artist who sees the appearance of the snow in the sunshine as a rich yellow rather than as the white which his theory tells him he ought to see."[15]

Yet, though phenomenology is pure observation in the above two senses, there is, for Peirce, no observation without the directing focus of meanings. Phenomenology, for Peirce, consists strictly in the observation and classification of whatever seems to be before the mind at any given time. It provides the "ultimate analysis of experience." In order to classify and analyze, there must first be the creative formation of meaningful structures that provide the delineations for classifications and the tools of analysis. Interpretive, legislative elements must enter into the phenomenological focus on experience as it appears in order for an "observing" mind to grasp and delineate its pervasive textures. This point is well summarized in Peirce's claim that "It is the genius of the mind, that takes up all these hints of sense, adds immensely to them, makes them precise, and shows them in intelligible form."[16] Within the context of Peirce's radical rejection of the spectator theory of knowledge, it is not possible to focus on any aspect of experience independently of interpretive elements. There are, then, highly interpretive elements at work in Peirce's phenomenology as the "pure observation" of what appears as it appears. From this backdrop the following discussion will turn to the experiential elements involved in his so-called transcendental strain or his "logical deduction" of the categories.

That Peirce was strongly influenced by Kant is undeniable, but this does not lead to some version of a transcendental deduction of the categories. Here, as elsewhere, Peirce's Kantianism is a radically transformed pragmatic version, and it rules out both intuitionism and formalism. This point can best be developed by first turning to Peirce's own account of his relationship to Kant and to his more Kantian sounding claims.

Peirce observes that since Kant, the importance of systems being constructed architectonically has been recognized, yet the full significance of this has not been adequately apprehended.[17] He clarifies this point via a critique of past philosophical systems in which, "an idea which has been found interesting and fruitful has been adopted, developed, and forced to yield explanations of all sorts of phenomena. Just as if a man, being seized with the conviction that paper was a good material to make things of, were to go to work to build a papier mâché house."[18] Meanwhile, the remaining systems of philosophy have consisted of reforms, sometimes quite radical, in light of problems found within an accepted position. But, he states, "this is like partially rebuilding a house."[19] Peirce then goes on to correct this misapprehension by continuing his analogy:

> When a man is about to build a house, what a power of thinking he has to do before he can safely break ground. With what pains he has to excogitate the precise wants that are to be supplied! What a study to ascertain the most available and suitable materials, to determine the mode of construction to which those ma-

> terials are best adapted, and to answer a hundred such questions. Now without riding the metaphor too far, I think we may safely say that the studies preliminary to the construction of a great theory should be at least as deliberate and thorough as those that are preliminary to the building of a dwelling house.[20]

Peirce's specific recommendation for those who wish to form an opinion about fundamental problems of philosophy is that they should examine all areas of human knowledge so that they understand the nature of the materials a philosophical theory must concern itself with and, only then, turn to the nature of philosophical problems and the best way of solving them.[21] And his point concerning this type of empirical survey is geared toward the specific recommendation that one engage in a systematic study of the conceptions and their interrelation and uses that are capable of building a good philosophic theory.[22] After looking at many different disciplines and giving a brief "hint at their nature" in providing conceptions "serviceable for philosophy," Peirce turns to the examination of logic and finds analogous conceptions. Any phenomenological survey must include a phenomenological examination of logic, for, as Peirce states in a letter to James, phenomenology is the analysis of "what kind of constituents there are in our thoughts and lives," taking thoughts in the logical sense that has "nothing to do with psychology."[23] In turning to his phenomenological focus on what constituents there are in our thoughts, he states that

> Among the many principles of Logic which find their application in Philosophy, I can here only mention one. Three conceptions are perpetually turning up at every point in every theory of logic, and in the most rounded systems they occur in connection with one another. They are conceptions so very broad and consequently indefinite that they are hard to seize and may be easily overlooked. I call them the conceptions of First, Second, Third.[24]

Recognizing the tentative and vague nature of the experiences that give rise to the abductive generation of the categories, Peirce can express the wish that in the future students retrace the ground he has covered and present their results to the community.[25]

Only in light of such a vague and empirically grasped recognition of these distinct conceptions can Peirce abductively create the interpretive structure that allows him to claim that "We find then a priori that there are three categories of undecomposable elements to be expected in the phaneron: those which are simply positive totals, those which involve dependence but not combination, those which involve combination."[26] This is not a Kantian fixed a priori; rather this claim is "a priori" in that although it is abductively generated in the light of past experience it is logically prior to the analysis of ongoing experience. It is a tool created to bring to experience for the interpretation of experience, one that can be discarded for another if it does not adequately work and is thus like the conditional or hypothetical certitudes of mathematics. As he stresses, phenomenology, as a science which does not "aim to declare that something is positively or categorically true . . . must, if it is to be properly grounded, be made to depend upon the Conditional or Hypothetical Science of Pure Mathematics,[27] whose only aim is to discover not how things actually are, but how they might be supposed to be."[28] The tool dictates what we must find if we use it; *if* we use it, *then* certain things must follow, for it legislates the interpretation of experience. But it may be found to be pragmatically useless, in that too much of experience cannot be incorporated into it. Thus, after asserting the "a priori" nature of the categories, Peirce is led immediately to suggest, "Now let us turn to the phaneron and see what we find in fact."[29] And, he stresses that in turning to the phaneron, each of the categories has to find its justification in its usefulness within experience,[30] for they cannot be regarded as final "as Kant thought" but must be put to the test by an independent examination of the facts.[31]

Peirce, then, can emphatically point out the uselessness of transcendentalism,[32] yet hold to an a priori dimension in the formulation of the categories, for there is a dimension that legislates the manner in which we focus on experience. Like all interpretive tools, the categories of phenomenology arise out of experience but in turn legislate the analysis of experience. They are not handed down from on high, nor are they pure inductions from experience; they are a creative, interpretive framework through which to focus on the entire gamut of "whatever is in any way present to mind." Thus it is that Peirce can claim that, with his interactional, synechistic understanding of subjective-objective, the issue of the a priori "gains new life."[33]

It is in the context of these dynamics that Peirce's partial agreement with Kant concerning congenital tendencies of the mind in relation to the categories must be understood.[34] Indeed, Peirce goes so far as to hold that the pragmatist cannot deny a doctrine of innate ideas.[35] Contrary to traditional notions of them, however, Peirce's pragmatic transformation of innate ideas or congenital tendencies of mind does not indicate absolute structures. What he means by this claim is that the pragmatist must hold to the embeddedness within behavior of dispositional tendencies, which are for him, of course, the core of interpretive structures. Dispositional tendencies, however, are always "tendencies in relation to" or a "readiness" in relation to "given circumstances."[36] Thus, what is emphasized by innate ideas or congenital tendencies is the pragmatic interplay of interpretive categories and the conditions of their formation and retention.

The "a priori" categorial set is not something fixed, final, or absolute. Rather it is a tool, which though in being applied is legislative, is itself further developed or refined in the very process of legislating, for its adequacy must be continually tested by future observations. As Peirce states, the materials supplied by the categories must be able "to predict many more things which new observations can alone bring to the test."[37] These new situations both serve to verify, and to demand revision of, the categories.

These experimental dynamics can be well exemplified by turning more directly to the relation of the categories to Peirce's analysis of logic. Though this relationship is generally held to point toward the "formalist" strain of his thought, a brief sketch of its history points toward the ongoing pragmatic, processive, open-ended nature of categorial determination developed above.

Peirce's interest in the interactive relationship among three irreducible conceptions is something he brought to his understanding of logic. Indeed this was already developed in 1861 in terms of the I, It, and Thou.[38] And, in an 1866 paper Peirce relates the I, It, and Thou to the three references of a sign. As Murray Murphey well observes concerning that paper, it "suggests that the terms 'Firstness,' 'Secondness,' and 'Thirdness' were first derived from the names of the pronouns and only later matched with the number of entities connected by the relations."[39]

Further, in his ongoing development and revision of the categories, culminating in his revised list of categories presented in 1885 in the paper "One, Two Three: Fundamental Categories of Thought and of Nature," which views the categories squarely in terms of monadic, dyadic, and triadic logical relations, the continuity of terminology tended to hide the substantive changes taking place. Thus Murphey claims that while "Extensive revisions of position pass unnoticed under a shell of changeless terminology," the revision of the categories was in fact so substantial that new names should have been provided to avoid confusion.[40] It would seem that Peirce's triadic divisions influenced the way he approached mathematical/logical issues. Yet, in their application to this area, to be verified by their workability, the early categories legislated, were found inadequate, and as a result were altered, partially in a substantive sense, partially in the sense of a clarification and sharpening of originally too vague intentions.[41] Also, though it was not until 1885 that Peirce distinguished formal and material aspects of the categories, this lack of distinction in the earlier categories, far from pointing toward their pure formality, is indicative of the inseparable intermingling of the two dimensions. Peirce's writings point to the fact that the impetus for his ongoing revision of the categories was not only discoveries in logical theory but also problems connected with his theories of cognition and reality. Recognizing the difficulty of this ongoing project, Peirce states, "I will endeavor to convey to you some idea of the conceptions themselves. It is to be remembered that they are excessively general ideas, so very uncommonly general that it is far from easy to get any but a vague apprehension of their meaning."[42]

It would seem that Peirce's three categories brought into significant focus in a general sense the new observations involved in examining the logic of relatives, yet they were revised because of their inability to adequately deal with this new area under examination. And there is of course a big difference between revising the categories in light of their inadequacy to accommodate the new data of the logic of relatives and the claim that they are *deduced from* the logic of relatives.[43] David Savan points out that Peirce clearly vacillates as to whether to rest logic upon observation or to rest observation upon logical procedures, and that "Peirce is tempted to suggest that the issue is only verbal." Yet this issue, Savan continues, is "so central to his thought that he cannot accept this escape, even as a last resort."[44] What Peirce did not adequately see was that no clear-cut answer could be given because of the dynamic interplay between the two. The categories are derived from experience yet are legislative for the analysis of experience, while at the same time subject to revision in light of experience.

These experimental dynamics hold in the area of logic as well as in all other areas of experience. Developments in any area of human experience are brought into focus through the categories but may themselves demand categorial revision. This is not a vicious circle but an exemplification of the cumulative process involved in the pragmatic, experimental interplay between meanings and experience.

Phenomenology, precisely as experimental phenomenology, displays this pragmatic interplay. What is involved in the experimental nature of phenomenology is an organization of experience in ways which work in grasping universally pervasive tones or textures of what appears as it appears, tones or textures that are continually put to the test in future observation of phenomena. These categories that work have arisen through the creativity of abductive processes based in part on the thorough study of the various disciplines to obtain a "hint at their nature" and, once developed, can be applied back to these disciplines in forms and terminologies relevant to each, though in their very application they are subject to the test of continual workability.[45]

The failure to recognize Peirce's halting and never clearly defined use of the above method leads to the often raised question as to whether he was attempting an empirical justification of the categories or an a prior deduction of them. If a dichotomy is made in this way, then the problems attributed to Peirce's method do in fact arise. If the method is empirical, then we cannot know that the categories have universal application. Alternately, if the method reduces to a rational assertion, they have universal application "by fiat" but seem somewhat arbitrary in their application to experience.[46]

The vague recognition of some of the features of Peirce's halting, never clearly defined pragmatic, experimental method involved in categorial inquiry leads Dewey to note that Peirce's analysis of the phaneron has a logical dimension to it.[47] Similarly, Thomas Goudge points out that "in reality Peirce's phaneroscopy is a double-edged sword, possessing at once both its rational and empirical edge."[48] It is precisely Peirce's pragmatic interrelation of "rational" and "empirical" factors in his phenomenology that is incorporated in the dynamic interplay between meanings abductively formulated and legislative for experience, and the vague experiences that give rise to them and that, as made precise through these interpretive or legislative tools, serve to judge them adequate or inadequate.[49]

If, as Peirce holds, the dynamics of experimental method allow for alternative interpretations, which are continually open and subject to revision, then he must allow for the possibility of alternatives to the categories of Firstness, Secondness, and Thirdness. This, indeed, is precisely what he does hold. Peirce nowhere indicates that his categories are absolute or eternal, and in fact he states quite clearly that though his selection may probably be the most adequate, alternative series of categories are possible.[50] Or, as he elsewhere states of his categories, "I do not claim nor opine that this set comprises all indecomposable[51] and almost universally recurring ideas, but merely that it is *one* such set having a peculiar importance of its own, perhaps, on the whole, greater than that of any other set."[52] Again, he notes that at every step "conceptions are met with which presumably do not belong to this series of ideas."[53] Indeed, as to his three universal categories of Firstness, Secondness, and Thirdness, there is perhaps "no very good reason for thinking that they are more universal than the others."[54]

It may here be objected that Peirce's frequent emphasis on the possibility of alternative categorial sets, while indicative of his fallibilism, does not involve pluralism. Thus, one might argue that a doctrine of categories, *if* correct, would be definitively and uniquely so. Yet pluralistic implications are contained in the fact that Peirce can claim that his set of categories is probably the *most* adequate and, at the same time, *also* claim that not only are alternative series of categories possible, but "at every step" features are encountered that do not fit his categories or "series of ideas," for his set does not "comprise" all. And, since his set may well be the *most* adequate, but yet does not comprise all, presumably by their very nature categorial sets *cannot* do so, thus allowing for alternative possibilities. Even the most adequate set of categories will not rule out the possibility of grasping the phenomenon in different ways that work in grasping features that overflow the bounds of those categorial distinctions. It has been seen that what one finds is partially dependent upon what one brings, and alternative ways of bringing will lead to different discriminations within the rich textures of the phenomena. Some ways of discriminating within the phaneron are better than others, but none can be exhaustive of its richness, and other categorial sets may be "equally universal." Peirce's experimental phenomenology, then, not only is fallibilistic, but incorporates an inherent pluralism, for there are in theory always alternative, perhaps equally adequate, perhaps better, ways of organizing the phenomena because of the creative abstractive nature of the categories and the richness of the phaneron.

The discussion thus far has focused on the development of Peirce's categories through a pragmatically oriented "experimental phenomenology." It is now time to turn to an examination of Peirce's move from the categories as phenomenologically descriptive of the textures, tones, or tints of experience to the categories as metaphysically assertive of reality, and to the dynamic experimental nature of this move, which both founds the speculative categorial claims of metaphysics and gives further confirmation to the adequacy of the categories as phenomenological.

Peirce holds that "Metaphysics is founded in phenomenology but goes beyond it." The nature of this "going beyond" is found in his posing of the "problem of metaphysics": "We must begin by asking whether the categories can be admitted as simple and irreducible conceptions; and afterward to go on to ask whether they cannot all be supposed to be real constituents in the universe."[55] His conclusion seems evident from his statement that the "premisses of nature . . . though they are not the perceptual facts that are premisses to us, nevertheless must resemble them in being premisses. We can only imagine what they are by comparing them with premisses for us."[56] This stress on analogy with perceptual facts in the move to metaphysics is important in two respects. First, experience of perceptual facts, while manifesting the three categorial features found in all experience, are that special part of experience that serve as signs of an independently real universe, and metaphysics "endeavors to comprehend the Reality of Phenomena."[57] Second, it would seem that perhaps Peirce's metaphysical discussions of the three categories and their interrelation can best be understood by constant reference to some analogue to be found in his understanding of perceptual awareness, a point that will be pursued further in the following chapter.

Peirce can give an affirmative answer to the above posed question concerning the "problem of metaphysics" because there is, for him, no gap between the categories as phenomenological and as ontological, for there is no gap between experience and reality.[58]

The epistemic and ontological unity at the heart of experience is expressed by Peirce in a telling criticism of Kant: "That time and space are innate ideas, so far from proving that they have merely a mental existence, as Kant thought, ought to be regarded as evidence of their reality. For the constitution of the mind is the result of evolution under the influence of experience."[59] Indeed, Peirce's pragmatic transformation of the doctrine of innate ideas that points, as indicated above, to the nature of the dynamics of phenomenological inquiry, points even more directly to the interrelation of the categories as phenomenological and as metaphysical. For dispositional tendencies are tendencies of a concrete organism in interaction with a natural universe, and it is this epistemic and ontological interactional unity that is ultimately emphasized by Peirce's pragmatic, dynamic understanding of innate ideas.

What appears within experience, then, is also the appearance of the independently real; there is no ontological gap between appearance and reality. As Peirce observes, "Synechism . . . will not admit a sharp sundering of phenomena and substrates. That which underlies a phenomenon and determines it thereby is, itself, in a measure, a phenomenon."[60] Further, it is at the same time "to me" to whom it appears and reflects my intentional link with the externally real. Thus Peirce can say that "Perhaps it may reconcile the psychologist to the admission of perceptual judgments involving generality to be told that they are perceptual judgments concerning our own purposes."[61] The epistemic and ontological unity of these two dimensions can be seen from Peirce's position that, though the generality of perceptual judgments reflects our own purposes, "since no cognition of ours is absolutely determinate, generals must have a real existence."[62] For Peirce, these are "two sides of the same shield."[63] Or, as he eloquently summarizes his position, though "everything which is present to us is a phenomenal manifestation of ourselves," this "does not prevent its being a phenomenon of something without us, just as a rainbow is at once a manifestation both of the sun and of the rain."[64] The general features manifest in the phenomenological dimensions of experience and embodied in the categories of phaneroscopy not only permeate the structure of our meanings but at once throw us onto the reality within which we are embedded. Or, as Peirce states, the "list of categories" is "applicable to being."[65]

To further explore the nature of the categories for Peirce, the discussion will turn to the issue of just what the metaphysical categories are intended to be "about." Or, in Peirce's terminology, what is one talking about when one talks of "truths of being?"[66] This problem can best be met by a somewhat negative approach. What Peirce's pragmatism will not allow should by now be evident. As he states, pragmatism serves to warn us "that almost every proposition of ontological metaphysics is either meaningless gibberish—one word being defined by other words, and they by still others, without any real conception ever being reached—or else is downright absurd."[67] Thus, if metaphysical discussion is to be of value it must be not about empty words but about meaningful concepts. In speaking of empty words, Peirce points out that

> Certain very metaphysical and eminently intellectual notions are absolutely simple. But though these concepts cannot be defined by genus and difference, there is another way in which they can be defined. All determination is by negation; we can first recognize any character only by putting an object which possesses it into comparison with an object which possesses it not. A conception, therefore, which was quite universal in every respect would be unrecognizable and impossible.[68]

And "being" is precisely such an "unrecognizable and impossible concept," for as Peirce states, "Being . . . may be defined, for example, as that which is common to the objects included in any class, and to the objects not included in the same class. But this is nothing new to say that metaphysical conceptions are primarily and at bottom thoughts about words."[69] Or, as Peirce more succinctly sums up his views on "being": "The conception of being, therefore, plainly has no content."[70] Thus, it can be seen that being, for Peirce, is an "empty concept," or, in more exact terms, "being" is not a concept at all, merely a term to which we can give no meaning, for, as indicated above, a concept to which no empirical content can be given is, in fact, no concept at all. Metaphysics, then, is not about "being qua being" but about *categories of* being, which is quite another matter. Thus, he states that "there are three *modes* of being," which are manifested phenomenologically.[71] Peirce's statement that the materials supplied by Firstness, Secondness, and Thirdness can account "for the main features of the universe as we know it,"[72] is perhaps more true to his intentions than his statement that the categories are "applicable to being."

The categories indicate not distinct realms of being but discernible features that help in understanding the interrelated characteristics of the universe in which we are embedded.

These metaphysical categories involve neither spectator attempts to grasp reality "as it is" independently of our modes of interpreting nor related attempts to transcend our perspectival condition by a move to an absolute perspective that somehow contains all other perspectives. Rather, they are products of creative, abductive attempts to articulate features of reality in a way that can accommodate the various tones or textures to which we are attuned. Like all interpretive tools, the metaphysical categories are perspectival and subject to revision in terms of their workability in accounting for features of reality that intrude within experience and pervade the tones and textures of experience. Peirce's mode of eliciting the phenomenological categories and his subsequent application of them to metaphysical reality indicates an awareness of this. In the last analysis, however, Peirce confounds the independence of reality as it intrudes within experience with our workable interpretations of it. This confusion is evinced in his statement that "Metaphysics is the science of Reality. Reality consists in regularity. Real regularity is active law . . . Thirdness."[73] Thus, "metaphysics, as I have just remarked, treats of phenomena in their Thirdness."[74] Peirce then goes to deliberate pains to elaborate a metaphysics that gives equal pay to Firstness, Secondness, and Thirdness.[75]

The above clarification shows that Peirce's argument commits the fallacy of equivocation. In one sense reality is an affair of Thirdness, for it is only through interpretive concepts or categories that there is an objective reality *as known*, be it the reality grasped by the metaphysician or the reality of commonsense objects and facts as the outcome of our everyday perceptual judgments. And concepts and categories are best characterized as exemplifications of Thirdness. To understand this interpretive process, however, Peirce considers independent reality to be characterized by Firstness, Secondness, and Thirdness. Peirce's equivocation here helps clarify the two distinct concepts of reality that pervade his writings in general,[76] the reality with which perception begins and the reality with which it ends;[77] that is, the real in its independence of human noetic activity[78] and the categorized reality with its known objective properties, reality as the "end product" of the interpretive perceptual process.[79] Thus, reality for Peirce is both that which is independent of what anybody may think,[80] and that which will be an object represented in the ultimate opinion of mankind.[81]

In light of the above discussion, it can be seen that while metaphysics is dependent upon phenomenology and hence on the categories phenomenology establishes, metaphysical claims concerning the realities represented by its own categories legislate, and must prove adequate for the analysis of, the experience of reality. Further, the adequacy of the metaphysical categories in their own right gives added verification to the categories of phenomenology in which they are grounded. Thus, though metaphysics presupposes phenomenology for its categories, the adequacy of the metaphysical categories, which are verified through the intelligibility they introduce into our experiences of the real, helps verify the adequacy of the phenomenological categories. If the categories are inadequate for metaphysics, they are inadequate for phenomenology, for reality appears in the phenomena, though in focusing on the phenomena it is not judged as reality. Peirce's metaphysical claims, then, are rooted in the phenomenological interpretive descriptions of experience and help verify their adequacy. There is an experimental dynamics operative in the articulation of the phenomenological categories, in the development of the metaphysical categories, and in the relation between the phenomenological and metaphysical categories. The fallibilism and pluralism indicated above in Peirce's "experimental phenomenology" holds mutatis mutandis for the metaphysical context that it founds.

At this point, one may object that Peirce's position seems to have become involved in an arbitrary circle with no firm roots anywhere. It is true that though his metaphysics attempts to understand the independent element that enters, along with a conceptual element, into our sense of empirical reality, what this independent element is like can be determined only from within experience; and it is also true that how we understand our experience will in part be influenced by the ontological categories in terms of which we approach it. Such a self-corrective method is not viciously circular, however, nor is it circular at all; it is a cumulative process based on the pragmatic interplay at every level between concepts or categories and experience. Our interpretive concepts and categories at all levels have arisen out of past experience and have been made prescriptive for the interpretation of future experience. This type of mutual feedback is surely not arbitrary; indeed it harmonizes quite well with the conception of scientific method as indicating a self-corrective rather than a "building block" enterprise. It is to the scientific as well as metaphorical nature of metaphysics that the discussion will now turn.

Peirce holds that the attitude of metaphysics "toward the universe is nearly that of the special sciences from which it is mainly distinguished, by confining itself to such parts of physics and psychics as can be established without special means of observation. But these are very peculiar parts, extremely unlike the rest."[82] According to Buchler, "What these 'peculiar parts' are we never find expatiated in Peirce."[83] And, in the too frequently asserted claims of the supposed "scientism" of Pierce's position,[84] the peculiarity of metaphysics seems to be virtually ignored. Though it is true that Peirce never explicitly clarifies this point, he perhaps gives the clue to their peculiarity in his statement that metaphysics "rests upon a kind of phenomena with which every man's experience is so saturated that he usually pays no particular attention to them."[85] Thus, the data for metaphysics differ from those of science precisely because the former are so pervasive of our every experience that their presence is often not recognized. This difficulty can be dealt with through the painstaking method of experimental phenomenology, which provides, ultimately, a clearer focus on the data from which metaphysics begins.

We see then that metaphysics, like science, rests upon observation. This, however, does not mean that metaphysical assertions are open to direct verification in experience. As Peirce points out, even "the things that any science discovers are beyond the reach of direct observation. . . . It is only the premisses of science, not its conclusions,[86] which are directly observed."[87] It is enough for the experimental character of a science that its conceptions and theories are necessary for a more satisfactory explanation of certain phenomena that are directly observed.[88] Thus, the conclusions of neither metaphysics nor science are directly observed in experience. In metaphysics, "conclusions" or theories result from speculative extrapolation from the pervasive textures of experience.

Peirce observes that the assumption that underlies metaphysics is not so different than the assumption that underlies the possibility of scientific success, for "All the categories portend to" is to "suggest a way of thinking; and all the possibility of science depends upon the fact that human thought necessarily partakes of whatever character is diffused through the whole universe, and that its natural modes have some tendency to be the modes of action of the universe."[89] Anticipating a possible objection here he observes, "I hear you say: 'This smacks too much of an anthropomorphic conception.' I reply that every scientific explanation of a natural phenomenon is a hypothesis that there is something in nature to which the human reason is analogous."[90] Peirce states in speaking of anthropomorphism:

> I heartily embrace most of the clauses of that doctrine if some right of private interpretation be allowed to me. I hold, for instance, that man is so completely hemmed in by the bounds of his possible practical experience, his mind is so restricted by being the instrument of his needs, that he cannot, in the least, *mean* anything that transcends those limits. . . . For let him try ever so hard to think anything about what is beyond that limit, it simply cannot be done.[91]

Thus, that which transcends experience in either science or metaphysics is anthropomorphic in the sense that we can think of it only in terms of our experience. In both science and metaphysics, we proceed to hypothesis via analogy from experience to the conditions that account for it. Both science and metaphysics rest on observation but proceed to explanatory frameworks. Peirce prefers to say that science and metaphysics are anthropomorphic, but what he means is not that the "matter" of either science or metaphysics is of the nature of our experience but that we can understand it or even conceive of it only as in some way analogous to our experience.

Philip Wiener has aptly noted that Peirce "boldly generalized the role of imagination," making it the "source of all the sciences."[92] Imaginative, metaphorical thinking is involved in much more than science and metaphysics for Peirce, however. As he states, "Metaphysics has been said contemptuously to be a fabric of metaphors. But not only metaphysics, but logical and phaneroscopical concepts[93] need to be clothed in such garments."[94] And ultimately, for Peirce, metaphor is involved not just in the above disciplines but in the very fabric of thought, "Since there is no possibility of framing words, or conceptions either, unless it be in the most scanty and insufficient supply, otherwise than by metaphors founded on human conduct."[95] In Peirce's own metaphorical terms, "a pure idea without metaphor or other significant clothing is an onion without a peel."[96] This is to be expected, for it has been seen that Peirce's pragmatic transformation of Kant unifies understanding, sensation, and imagination in the creative functioning of meaning as habit.[97] All awareness goes beyond what is given in experience, and thus, even "When I say to myself the stove is black, I am making a little theory to account for the look of it."[98] Metaphysical thought, like scientific thought, is continuous with the dynamics of commonsense perception. The imaginative flight of metaphysics does not form a tension with Peirce's pragmatic theory of meaning but rather arises from it. As Peirce insists:

> If pragmatism is the doctrine that every conception is a conception of conceivable practical effects, it makes conception reach far beyond the practical. It allows any flight of imagination, provided this imagination ultimately alights upon a possible practical effect; and thus many hypotheses may seem at first glance to be excluded by the pragmatical maxim that are not really so excluded."[99]

Because the data from which metaphysics sets out are the characteristics that pervade all experience, scientific and nonscientific alike, its conclusions must be more comprehensive and hence less verifiable than the conclusions of scientific theory, but the difference is not essentially one of kind. The difficulty of either formulating or verifying a metaphysical theory does not mean that metaphysical speculation will eventually halt. Peirce points out that "you might as well pass a law that no man shall jump over the moon, it wouldn't forbid him to jump just as high as he possibly could."[100] As he summarizes, we *need* to think of the universe as intelligible, and furthermore, we *shall* do so.[101] Nor *should* metaphysical speculation end, and Peirce takes his stand on this point with a question of his own: "Do you think, reader, that it is a positive fact that 'Truth, crushed to earth, shall rise again,' or do you think that this, being poetry, is only a pretty fiction?"[102] That metaphysical endeavor is rooted in human "need" and highly imaginative in nature does not detract from the intellectual urgency of its development, for "Find a scientific man who proposes to get along without any metaphysics and you have found one whose doctrines are thoroughly vitiated by the crude and uncriticized metaphysics with which they are packed."[103] Peirce sums up the problem of metaphysics thus: "The best that can be done is to supply an hypothesis, not devoid of all likelihood, in the general line of growth of scientific ideas, and capable of being verified or refuted by future observers,"[104] at least in some sense. Concerning his own positive metaphysics, Peirce states that he is "convinced that it would go far toward supplying the philosophy that is best to harmonize with physical science."[105]

In contrasting the metaphysical perspectives of Peirce and Whitehead, Victor Lowe notes that "Peirce's position seems to be a kind of scientism," while, for Whitehead, "Metaphysics is nothing but the description of the generalities which apply to all the details of practice."[106] According to the present view of Peirce's method of metaphysics, however, this latter characterization could well be attributed to him. It is precisely the point of Peirce's phenomenologically founded metaphysics that "everything of which we are conscious, as enjoyed, perceived, willed, or thought, shall have the character of a particular instance of the general scheme."[107] Perhaps it is just the awareness of this role, coupled with the recognition that metaphysical statements are speculative extrapolations from experience, that led Peirce to use such blatantly anthropomorphic language.[108]

Peirce's metaphysical discussions are couched in highly speculative, metaphorical, and anthropomorphic language not in spite of the nature and limits of meaningfulness imposed by his pragmatic epistemology but because of them. His metaphysical discussions are highly metaphorical precisely because he recognized them to be metaphorical or imaginative extrapolations from experience. As John E. Smith has aptly captured this point: "Peirce was acutely aware both of the extent to which metaphysics involves 'extrapolation' and of the unavoidability of this sort of reasoning if we are not to deceive ourselves concerning the ultimate assumptions behind what we believe."[109] It has been noted that Peirce's formulation of his ideas often "converts a perfectly reasonable doctrine into something which seems utterly outrageous."[110] And indeed if, on the one hand, Peirce's claim to be scientific in his metaphysics is taken too narrowly or, on the other hand, his metaphorical assertions are taken too literally, then his doctrines will seem outrageous and often contradictory.

The above examination has attempted to explore Peirce's pragmatic method, or method of experimental inquiry, as the context within which his doctrine of the categories can be interpreted. His method of categorical development reveals the experimental nature of phenomenology, of metaphysics, and of the relation between their respective claims. One can see in this development an exaggeration of the experimental method by which we have meaningful everyday experience. There is an exaggeration of the metaphorical, imaginative, creative features of the meanings that arise out of past experience through abductive fixations of experience and legislate for the analysis of future experience. Further, there is an exaggerated attentiveness to what appears in experience, to its pervasive features or textures, an attentiveness that both founds the categories and serves to verify their adequacy. And, as Peirce has been seen to point out, the claims of his experimental phenomenology, and hence the claims of the metaphysics that it grounds, are fallibilistic and open to alternative categorial possibilities. There is an inbuilt pluralism here that is not merely a step toward final agreement but is inescapable because of the concrete richness of the textures of experience, the abstractive nature of the classificatory focus required, and the creativity involved in obtaining this classificatory focus. It is because of both the fallibilism and the inherent pluralism that Peirce could claim that he received "the pleasure of praise" from what "was meant for blame," when, as he noted, "a critic said of me that I did not seem to be absolutely sure of my own conclusions."[111] The next chapter will examine Peirce's own metaphysical conclusions to reveal the metaphysical grounding for pluralism that they imply.

CHAPTER 5

Peirce's Pragmatic Metaphysics: The Foundation for Pluralism

An interpretation of Peirce's metaphysics implicitly permeates much of the interpretation of other areas of his thought, even by those who consider his metaphysics extraneous to what is of contemporary relevance in his philosophy. As John E. Smith so aptly observed and warned,

> Since Peirce took science seriously and frequently spoke disparagingly not only of 'seminary' philosophy in contrast with 'laboratory' philosophy but of much previous metaphysics as well, some have concluded that Peirce's own metaphysics may be dismissed as a mere decoration which need not be taken seriously. In the present upsurge of interest in Peirce's thought, moreover, one can detect signs of the same bias; it is expressed in the assumption that the 'real' Peirce is Peirce the logician and philosopher of science. Peirce the speculative philosopher, presumably, does not count. The fact is that such a view is not only erroneous as a description of the man and his thought, but it is short-sighted as well.[1]

More recently, Helmut Pape has expressed a similar observation and corresponding warning in pointing out that Peirce's evolutionary philosophy of nature and cosmology

> have not only been criticized—they have been made fun of or treated with contempt by important philosophers. . . . Quite to the contrary, Peirce's logic and semiotics have been taken seriously, praised and discussed in and out of philosophy departments. But his semiotics and his philosophy of nature are in fact very closely connected. I don't think that we should ignore Peirce's hypothesis that such a connection exists.[2]

According to the presumption of the present work, "Peirce the speculative philosopher" not only counts, not only should not be ignored, but is of central importance, for the entire interpretation of Peirce's pragmatic pluralism is interwoven with a particular interpretation of his metaphysics as its foundation. Not only does his pragmatism lead to his metaphysics,[3] but his metaphysics leads to his pragmatism. Thus, Peirce holds that his pragmatic analysis of experience implies the reality of universals, and he also claims that "Unless we had first been convinced that there *are* real generals, pragmaticism would never have entered our heads."[4]

The following preliminary remarks concerning Peirce's metaphysics are intended to anticipate the general thrust of what will be developed in this chapter. There is a peculiar lack, in Peirce's metaphysical categories, of any category of process. It has been seen in previous chapters that the sense of temporality is constituent in the very nature of experience. Thus the sense of temporality is the experiential character that accounts for the very possibility of, and must pervade the features of, Firstness, Secondness, and Thirdness as portrayed in Peirce's phaneroscopy. Yet the experience of durational flow does not emerge as the content of any phenomenological category for Peirce. As that experience that yields the possibility of his categories, it is discussed by him in brief and scattered contexts, but not in the context of his phenomenological analysis of experience. Perhaps it receives a hint in the context of his phenomenology when he criticizes Hegel for not recognizing that the present in general is not the most abstract but the most concrete, the "nearest to sense."[5] Again, in a letter to William James he states, "What you call 'pure experience' is not experience at all and certainly ought to have a name. . . . My 'phenomenon' for which I must invent a new word is very near your 'pure experience' but not quite *since I do not exclude time.*"[6] Peirce's phenomenology cannot exclude time, for "We are directly aware of the flow of time."[7] This awareness yields the sense of a temporal "thickness" in which "The present is half past and half to come."[8]

Similarly, Peirce does not develop an ontological category of process. Rather, process is the ontological characteristic that accounts for the features grasped by the categories of metaphysics. Process is not itself a categorial feature for Peirce's metaphysics but is implicitly that which is understood through categorial delineations of its features. Though process must be a metaphysical category, opposed, for example, to the metaphysical category of substance, yet the metaphysical categories will be seen to be *categories of* process, ways in which a rich processive universe functions, just as it was seen that Peirce's triadic categorial phenomenological divisions are distinctions made within the richness of temporal experience.[9]

Because the pervasive, fundamental role of process is not made adequately explicit in Peirce's development of the categorial features of reality, he has problems breaking out of traditional distinctions, or he fails to adequately utilize novel emerging distinctions. This results in his various attempts to understand his position in terms of the false alternatives based on an historical tradition of substance philosophy and spectator theory of knowledge. Before turning to the issue of these alternatives, the following discussion will first prepare the way by examining Peirce's category of Firstness.

In any discussion of Peirce's philosophy, Firstness is usually the most neglected of his categories. This, however, is not due to any unique clarity of the category of Firstness, for, as Isabel Stearn has well noted, "Firstness is without any doubt the most elusive of Peirce's categories."[10] Similarly, Christopher Hookway has noted that "Firstness is the hardest of the three (categories) to focus on clearly, and it prompts some of Peirce's less helpful metaphors."[11] Boler accurately summarizes the plight of Firstness in his claim that it "is certainly the least clear of the categories and the one that receives the least attention."[12] The reason for this neglect may well be that an explicit interpretation of Firstness is not considered as important for the overall thrust of Peirce's philosophy as are interpretations of his other categories. It is the contention of this work, however, that Firstness provides the key for ultimately understanding the strong thread of pragmatic pluralism that pervades and unifies much of Peirce's thought.[13]

In keeping with Peirce's movement from the features of experience to the categories of metaphysics, as explored in the previous chapter, perceptual awareness can be expected to provide a basis for understanding Peirce's diverse characterizations of Firstness as a category of metaphysics. Moreover, previous distinctions made among the various "layers" incorporated in the perceptual judgment in its narrow sense will again come to the fore, though in different terminology. Peirce's brief discussions that contain a more neutral language of qualia will serve well in a transitional move from epistemic and phenomenological interests to more cosmic concerns.

Peirce states of qualia that "There is a distinctive quale to every combination of sensations so far as it is really synthesized."[14] Further, "in quale-consciousness there is but one quality, but one element. It is entirely simple."[15] This, however, is not meant to imply that we build up perception from atomic qualia. It has already been seen that what is immediately recognized as given, though expressed in language, is epistemologically prior to language. And, what is given as the percept interpreted in the perceptual judgment in its narrow sense, or the immediate recognition of the percept, and then expressed in the language of appearing or seeming, is not a "collection" of atomic qualia but a gestalt or relation of qualia. Our immediate recognition of the given, as the indubitable content of experience, is not that of atomic qualia. Rather, the recognized content is a unitary percept of "feeling tone," which, Peirce holds, has its own distinctive quale, a unitary quale or experienced content, which is analyzed rather than synthesized in the process of recognition. As Peirce observes, "We are, of course, directly aware of positive sense qualities in the percept (although in the percept they are in no wise separated from the whole object)."[16] Murphey's characterization incorporates these features when he notes that

> A First is not the same as what is usually called a percept . . . which has a structure and which combines a number of sense qualities. A pure First . . . is simple and devoid of structure. But every percept has a First which is the single impression created by the total ensemble of its elements. Moreover, if a single sense quality of a percept is prescinded from all the rest and is considered by itself, such a quality is a First.[17]

Peirce claims that "Each quale is in itself what it is for itself, without reference to any other. . . . Nevertheless, comparing consciousness does pronounce them to be alike. They are alike to the comparing consciousness, though neither alike nor unlike in themselves."[18] The repeatability of qualia, then, is itself a product of the synthesizing activity of consciousness acting upon unique qualia. The more fundamental level of unique qualia gives significance to Peirce's statement that "Firstness is predominant, not necessarily on account of the abstractness of that idea, but on account of its self-containedness. It is not in being separated from qualities that Firstness is most predominant, but in being something peculiar and idiosyncratic."[19] Qualia "in themselves" as "absolutely simple" and "absolutely free"[20] are "what the world was to Adam on the day he opened his eyes to it . . . that is first present, immediate, fresh, new, initiative, original, spontaneous, free."[21]

Such a characterization leads Peirce to speak of Firstness in terms of qualities of feeling.[22] As he analogously states, "There is no resemblance at all in feeling, since feeling is whatever it is, positively and regardless of anything else, while the resemblance of anything lies in the comparison of that thing with something else."[23] Murray Murphey distinguishes between the description of a First in epistemological terms and in psychological terms. Epistemically it is a sense quality, while psychologically it is a feeling, and "Peirce switches from one mode of description to the other with such abruptness that it is often difficult to tell which he is using unless one keeps this duality continually in mind."[24] To think of feeling as used by Peirce in terms of psychology, however, is to be misled by a word, for as Peirce himself emphatically states, "If by 'psychology' we mean the positive or observation science of the mind or consciousness . . . psychology can teach us nothing of the nature of feeling, nor can we gain knowledge of any feeling by introspection, for the very reason that it is our immediate consciousness." Or, as he elsewhere states, he uses the word *feeling* "to denote that which is supposed to be immediately, and all at one instant, present to consciousness." Peirce's use here of "supposed to be" emphasizes that we cannot directly observe what is instantaneously present to consciousness.[25]

Feeling, for Peirce, indicates an epistemic level, not a psychological content. It indicates that level of the experience of Firstness that is prior to the grasp of repeatable sense qualities. Feeling thus indicates that which is in its purity "unknowable." Though no element of the phaneron exists in isolation, even the "conceptual isolation" of pure Firstness for purposes of analysis is difficult because of its primitive nature. Peirce stresses that every description of it must be false to it.[26] A metaphorical or anthropomorphic extrapolation[27] from this claim concerning the "felt" character of qualitative immediacy to the claim that the "secondary qualities" are to be found in nature leads Peirce to his cryptic statement, usually taken as indicative of his idealism, that "It is a psychic feeling of red without us which arouses a sympathetic feeling of red in our senses."[28]

This level of felt qualitative immediacy is the important level for the issue at hand, for if qualia are unique in the most primitive experience of them, and if it is "comparing consciousness" that makes them repeatable, then Firstness in its metaphysical aspect does not seem to indicate any sort of determinate repeatables.[29] To allow the repeatability of qualia to lead to a metaphysics that gives an independent ontological status in any sense to determinate repeatables is completely to ignore this most basic mode of Firstness as it enters into experience. Thus, in turning to the example "Yesterday I saw a blue color; and here is a blue color," Peirce stresses that "some beginner may object that they have both blueness in them; but I reply that blueness is nothing but the idea of these sensations and of others I have had, thrown together and indistinctly thought at once."[30] We cannot compare presentations in terms of the ontological quality, "blueness," for the repeatable quality is itself dependent upon the assimilation of past and present presentations. Firstness as determining a class of repeatable qualitative presentations is the product of an epistemic function; it is not an ontological given. This epistemic function can be seen to be what was earlier expressed as the interpretive, assimilative role of the ponecipuum as the sensory core of the schematic image and as the basis for the perceptual judgment in its narrow sense.[31]

But even the unity of a unique "self-contained" quale has lost some of the original diversity, for as Peirce notes: "That very same logical element of experience, the quale-element, which appears upon the inside as unity, when viewed from the outside is seen as variety."[32] And, again, "No unity can originate in concentration . . . but any unity there [*sic*] was there already may in that way, be many times intensified."[33] And, since an uninterpreted quale is itself a "synthesis of sensations," then surely at this level also, what is seen on the inside as unity will be seen on the outside as variety. It would seem to be this aspect of Firstness that meets the characterization of it as something reached "by negation: one comes to a certain threshold in the inspection of experience and must jump off, so to speak, to posit the possibility of a primeval sensation."[34] Here, however, it is crucial to note that although Peirce uses the terms *impression* or *sensation* quite often, he explicitly indicates not only that there are no first impressions of sense,[35] but also that when he does use the term *impression* it is used to express a limiting concept to indicate the boundary of consciousness.[36] The concept of a synthesis of impressions as the limiting concept of the boundary of consciousness merges with the concept of the point of organism environment interaction. It throws us outward onto the universe within which perception arises. Just as recognition unifies diverse qualia, so qualia unify diverse stimuli.[37] And, just as the unifying function of recognition must have some basis upon which to work—however vague this basis may be—so the unifying function of the "production" of qualia must have some objective basis, no matter how vague, upon which to work. Peirce emphasizes this objective basis in his observation that "No sensation nor sense faculty is requisite for the possibility which is the being of the quality."[38] From the backdrop of the above transition to Firstness as a category of metaphysics, the discussion will now turn more directly to the character of Firstness as indicative of both ontological qualitative richness and ontological possibility.[39]

Here certain terminological confusions must be clarified. Peirce, in his writings, uses the term *possibility* to characterize not only Firstness but also Thirdness. Further adding confusion, he indiscriminately interchanges the terms *possibility* and *potentiality.* Peirce's dual use of the term *possibility* is quite understandable, for since Secondness comprises the domain of the actual, the possible, in a broad sense, must include both Firstness and Thirdness. What Peirce means, however, can be clarified in the light of a few illuminating statements. He holds that "A quality is how something may or might have been. A law is how an endless future must continue to be."[40] Again, at times he characterizes his three categories of being as possibility, actuality, and destiny.[41] Finally, he states that "Generality is either of that negative sort which belongs to the merely potential, as such, and this is peculiar to the category of Firstness, or it is of the positive kind which belongs to conditional necessity, and this is peculiar to the category of law."[42] What the contextual meaning of the various pairs of terms used to characterize Firstness and Thirdness indicates in each of these examples is that Firstness involves a weaker type of possibility than does Thirdness. The most appropriate terms to distinguish the possibility involved in each of the two categories would be *possibility,* to indicate the First category, and *potentiality* to indicate the Third category. However, because Peirce indiscriminately switches back and forth between these two terms, the present essay would often be using one term precisely where Peirce is stressing the other term.

To avoid such confusion, the term *negative possibility* and *positive possibility* will be used to characterize the possibility involved in Firstness and Thirdness respectively, though what will be meant by these terms is roughly the distinction between mere possibility and potentiality, or, in Peirce's terms, the difference between "a mere may-be"[43] and a "would-be."[44] This terminological distinction lies implicit in Peirce's claim that "Potentiality is the absence of Determination (in the usual broad sense) not of a mere negative kind but a positive capacity to be a Yea and to be a Nay."[45] Furthermore, this terminology has an advantage in its own right, for it will indicate clearly the relationship between possibility and generality.

The term *generality* must be clarified because it also serves a dual function. Peirce means by the general the opposite of the singular. Since the singular belongs to the category of Secondness, generality must, in a wide sense, characterize both Firstness and Thirdness. As indicated above, Peirce calls the generality of Firstness "negative generality" and the generality of Thirdness "positive generality." The meaning of these characterizations, however, can best be approached indirectly.

When the category of Firstness was discussed from the perspective of perceptual features, it was indicated that Firstness as constitutive of the universe would be characterized by diverse qualitative stimuli. However, to reveal the complexity that arises, a statement made by Peirce in connection with perception must be reintroduced here. As noted earlier in this chapter, though Peirce states that the quale element that appears on the inside as unity appears on the outside as variety,[46] he adds that "No unity can originate in concentration . . . but any unity there [*sic*] was there already may in that way, be many times intensified."[47] Thus, the ontological basis for the experience of Firstness is not merely "pure" Firstness or diverse qualitative stimuli in their aspect of diversity but pure Firstness "overlaid" with some unifying element. And if some element of unity within the diversity is required for the experience of Firstness in the sense of a unified quale, then this unity itself must be "part of" ontological Firstness. Thus, a further distinction between the element of diversity and the element of unity is necessary if Peirce's characterizations of Firstness are to be understood. This, however, leads straight to the problem of positive and negative generality.

Though recognizing the significance of Peirce's switch from substance to process in most areas, Boler states that "there is still a sense in which Peirce argues as Scotus does for a real common object."[48] "According to Peirce, the commonness of qualities, which interested the schoolmen, is but one form—a degenerate form at that—of real generality."[49] Thus, according to Boler, at one point at least real generality for Peirce indicates "real commonness" or repetition of form in some sense. Boler's argument seems to hinge on the unstated assumption that Peirce's ontological category of Firstness implies repeatable, fully structured qualities. On this assumption, since Peirce declares that Firstness involves generality, the "real generality" of Peirce's position, at this point at least, would be similar to the scholastic concept of the common nature as a "real common object." On this view, then, the degenerate or negative generality of Firstness provides a unifying factor by providing a rigid structuring of determinate repeatables. But questions remain. In what sense is this a negative or degenerate generality? Furthermore, did not Peirce's discussion of the epistemic and phenomenological dimensions of Firstness lead toward the expectation that the unity of diverse stimuli would be not a rigid structure of repetition but a somewhat indeterminate basis for a rigid epistemological structuring of repeatable qualities? However, this latter view appears to run into problems of its own, for it is not readily evident that Firstness as diverse qualitative stimuli can in any way be characterized as general. And, if the present interpretation is to find justification in Peirce's writings, then the real negative generality of Firstness must be accounted for.

What characterizes the general, as opposed to the singular, is the fact that the laws of excluded middle and noncontradiction do not apply to the general.[50] It would seem, then, that one could hold the diverse stimuli of the evolving universe, in their diversity, to be general in the negative sense that no determination can be made of them. Thus, though it is true that "a triangle in general is not isosceles nor equilateral; nor is a triangle in general scalene,"[51] yet a triangle in general is triangular, and the generality of triangularity does limit the possible alternatives of further determination. However, it would seem that the diverse stimuli, in their diversity, display a negative generality in that they are limited by nothing whatsoever. Peirce's reference to Firstness in this pure sense, which emphasizes the qualitative uniqueness of each of the stimuli, can be seen from his statement that "I cannot call it [Firstness] unity, for even unity supposes plurality."[52]

At this point, however, another problem arises, for the negative generality of Firstness has not accounted for the unifying element required by Peirce. The clue to the nature of this unity is found in Peirce's statement that "The general is seen to be precisely the continuous."[53] Generality, then, must involve continuity; hence, the generality of Firstness can only be fully understood when this category is viewed from the aspect of the unity or continuity that pervades it. Here it may be objected that continuity belongs to the category of Thirdness. Thus, it has been recently concluded that the close relationship between possibility and continuity is that of Firstness to Thirdness.[54] However, if the general is the continuous, then the negative generality of Firstness must imply a negative continuity, which belongs to the category of Firstness rather than Thirdness.[55] The negative continuity of Firstness, like negative generality, indicates a negative possibility or mere "may-be," which contains no positive possibility or "would-be" and which thus provides no positive range for further determinations. As Peirce states the position, "Firstness is essentially indifferent to continuity."[56]

Just as feeling was seen above to refer to that quale element, which in its purity can be related to nothing beyond itself, so the negative generality and continuity of Firstness, which forms the cosmological basis for our experience of qualia, can be related neither to what has been nor to what will be; it has no relatedness, it contains no "would-be." The importance of this continuity of Firstness can be seen in Peirce's claim that "Time as the universal form of change cannot exist unless there is something to undergo change and to undergo a change continuous in time there must be a continuity of changeable qualities."[57] Yet, Peirce characterizes such a qualitative continuity as that immediacy that mind has "practically extinguished,"[58] for mind separates and orders. That such qualities cannot be taken as subjective is evidenced through the bringing together of two claims by Peirce, "Not only is consciousness continuous in a subjective sense . . . its object is ipso facto continuous. In fact, this infinitesimally spread out consciousness is a direct feeling of its contents as spread out."[59] Furthermore, he states in reference to the "premisses of nature," which we "imagine" through comparison with our experience,[60] "As premisses, they must involve qualities."[61]

Peirce's discussion of Firstness as ontological possibility (as opposed to ontological generality) has frequently led to its identification with some type of Platonic essence.[62] This approach may at first glance seem a mere repetition, couched in different language, of the points made above in connection with Boler's analysis. However, this approach brings to light an entirely different aspect of the problem of interpreting Peirce's category of Firstness. W. P. Haas defends this "Platonic" line of interpretation, holding that "The possible seems to include for Peirce the universe of logical possibility or an ideal world. Some of these ideal, logical possibilities occur in the real world also. 'The sensible world is but a fragment of the ideal world.'"[63] And, notes Haas, Peirce insists that "the possible is a positive universe of being."[64] Peter Turley claims that the Platonic world is the locale of pure Firsts as qualities, thus combining elements of the interpretations offered by Boler and Haas.[65] Bertrand Helm, claiming that qualitative possibilities are not in time, similarly conflates qualitative possibilities with Platonic forms.[66]

Peirce, however, offers a clarification elsewhere that places these statements in a quite different light. He notes that "My old definition of the possible as that which we do not know not to be true (in some state of information real or feigned) is an anocoluthon. The possible is a positive universe . . . but that is all. Of course, there is a general logical possible . . . but there is also a possible which is something else."[67] This "possible which is something else" is a "positive universe of being." And this possible as a positive universe of being is the negative possibility of Firstness indicated above.[68]

It has been seen that the real possibility of Firstness is a negative possibility that must be carefully distinguished from the positive possibility of Thirdness and from the logical possibility that belongs in the discussion of epistemological issues. The real qualitative richness of Firstness is the richness of diverse qualitative stimuli that "contain" two distinct aspects, an aspect of total diversity and an aspect of somewhat indefinite unity, characterized by negative generality and negative continuity respectively. These two aspects of the qualitative richness are only analytically distinct, and together they constitute a continuum of qualitative diversity that is the very being of the negative possibility of Firstness. The category of Firstness thus indicates that reality is qualitatively rich, but that its qualitative richness indicates not a realm of sense universals or any sort of determinate repeatables but a realm of diverse and somewhat indefinite qualitative stimuli. There emerges from Peirce's epistemic/phenomenal characterization of Firstness in perception, then, a metaphysical category of Firstness that is neither a remnant of traditional conceptions of determinate repeatable qualities nor a remnant of traditional conceptions of eternal Platonic possibilities. Rather, what emerges is a Firstness that attributes to reality precisely those characteristics most antithetical to such traditional conceptions. Firstness in this sense not only underlies Peirce's radical rejection of foundationalist-antifoundationalist alternatives in epistemology, but also anticipates his rejection of the ontological alternatives offered by a tradition of substance metaphysics. The ensuing discussion will turn to this rejection of traditional ontological alternatives.

It has been suggested that "conditional idealism," "scholastic realism," and "pragmaticism" are only different names for Peirce's commitment to real possibility.[69] To this suggestion John Boler objects that as valuable as it is to see the interconnectedness of these doctrines, it seems a great mistake to neglect the richness of Peirce's thought as it is reflected in the three complementary approaches by viewing them all as somehow the same thing.[70] Both points of view have merit. Peirce's various approaches to his metaphysical doctrines indicate several important and real distinctions that he is attempting to delineate. However, when one philosopher can calmly proclaim to be an extreme realist, an idealist, and a pragmatist, it is perhaps time to pay somewhat less attention to avenues of approach and somewhat more attention to the terminus toward which they lead.

Because the relationship of Peirce's philosophy to idealism and realism yields both a tool for bringing to light important distinctions and an obstacle that stands in the way of understanding his own unique position, the following discussion will both examine in broad outlines Peirce's relationship to realism and idealism and attempt to briefly sketch his unique pragmatic metaphysics that emerges when these labels are discarded. In the following discussion, no attempt will be made to determine what is "really meant" by idealism or realism, for the important question is not the nature of the positions per se but the positions as Peirce understood them. If Peirce's interpretations of these positions are somewhat less than accurate, this fact is irrelevant for the present purpose. The following analysis will turn to his self-proclaimed idealism in order to explore the systematic significance of Peirce not being the idealist he claims to be.

To understand the significance of Peirce's self-proclaimed idealism within the context of his metaphysical system, it is helpful to view it not only in terms of the modifications he makes, but also—perhaps more so—in terms of the alternatives against which they are pitted. As Hjalmar Wennerberg has observed, Peirce's "arguments in favor of idealism are mainly of an apagogical nature; he tries to show that materialism is wrong."[71] This statement provides a first key for understanding the nature of Peirce's idealism, for, as will be seen, Peirce's most clear-cut assertions of idealism arise from a rejection of two other positions that he falsely thinks exhaust the possibilities. Indeed, the alternatives from which he begins are rooted in a tradition of substance and kinds of "stuff," while his search for an answer stems from an emerging framework of process and function.

Peirce regards materialism, idealism, and neutralism as three conflicting theories, each of which gives a definite answer to the question of the nature of the universe. He attempts to solve this problem by determining what kind of law governs the universe, physical law, or the law of the mind. That Peirce has expressed the alternatives in terms of laws rather than either ultimate substances or types of "stuff" may not at first seem a significant move, for the manner of operation of "mind stuff" would surely be different from the manner of operation of "material stuff." However, Peirce clearly indicates the nature of the problem for himself: "The distinction between psychical and physical phenomena *is* the distinction between final and efficient causation."[72] In short, Peirce is not asking the type of question provided by a substance metaphysics; he is asking a question concerning the behavior of the universe, and mind and matter are names of differing types of functions or processes operative in the universe. Peirce's question here can be seen to follow from his pragmatic orientation, which asserts that what a thing is, is determined by its activities or behavior, not by any underlying substance that determines or causes the behavior.

What, then, does Peirce intend by this distinction between final and efficient causation? He states that

> We must understand by final causation that mode of bringing facts about according to which a general description of result is made to come about, quite irrespective of any compulsion for it to come about in this or that particular way. . . . Final causation does not determine in what particular way it is to be brought about, but only that the result shall have a certain general character.[73]

One should not conclude from this that Peirce means by a final cause the same things as a purpose, for as he states almost immediately before the above passage, "a purpose is merely that form of final cause which is most familiar to our experience."

In contrast to final causation, efficient causation "is a compulsion determined by the particular condition of things, and is a compulsion acting to make that situation begin to change in a perfectly determinate way; and what the general character of the result may be in no way concerns the efficient causation."[74] Efficient causation is "stupid";[75] it is not Thirdness but Secondness.

With this initial clarification of the distinction between the law of mind and the law of matter, it is now time to turn to Peirce's analysis of the available choices. He points out that:

> The question arises whether psychical laws on the one hand and the physical law on the other are to be taken—
> (a) as independent, a doctrine often called monism but which I would name neutralism; or,
> (b) the psychical law as derived and special, the physical law alone as primordial, which is materialism; or,
> (c) the physical law as derived and special, the psychical law alone as primordial, which is idealism.[76]

Neutralism is rejected by Peirce because it assumes the existence of more independent elements than are necessary. "Monism" and "neutralism" both seem odd choices of terminology, for both Peirce's definition and rejection of the position indicate that what is involved is dualism, the irreducibility to two distinct "entities," mind and matter. One of his key objections to dualism as presented elsewhere, however, gives an insight into why he refers to it as monism or neutralism and to the direction in which he is headed. Peirce notes that

> Dualism in its broadest legitimate meaning as the philosophy which performs its analyses with an axe, leaving as the ultimate elements, unrelated chunks of being, this is most hostile to synechism. In particular, the synechist will not admit that physical and psychical phenomena are entirely distinct—whether as belonging to different categories of substance, or as entirely separate sides of one shield—but will insist that all phenomena are of one character, though some are more mental and spontaneous, others more material and regular. Still, all alike present that mixture of freedom and constraint, which allows them to be, nay, makes them to be teleological, or purposive.[77]

It can be seen from the above passage that dualism as "monism" is inadequate in that by completely separating reality into two types or chunks of being, it leaves each type operating according to a single law: the law of matter or the law of mind. It can further be seen from this passage that the separation of final and efficient causation as modes of behavior cannot be given the degree of separation at times indicated by Peirce's writings, and that the division of mental and physical simply in terms of final and efficient causation may in fact be inadequate in understanding Peirce's position. The "neutralism" of dualism can be seen to lie in the fact that primacy is given neither to the law of matter nor to the law of mind. In rejecting the neutralism of a dualistic position Peirce wants to give primacy to one law, and that law, of course, will be in some yet-to-be-determined sense, the "law of the mind."

Peirce's rejection of materialism gives further insight into the nature of his self-proclaimed idealism. Peirce argues against materialism by saying that "we know that when we try to verify any law of nature by experiment, we always find discrepancies between the observations and the theory. These we rightly refer to errors of observations, but why may there not be similar aberrations due to the imperfect obedience of the facts to the law?"[78] Peirce further holds that materialism "blocks the road to inquiry,"[79] since "Law is par excellence the thing that wants a reason."[80] Again, materialism cannot account for the many processes that are characterized by growth and increasing complexity, for the laws of mechanics are applicable only to processes that are reversible. Finally, in an appeal to commonsense experience, Peirce notes that "It is sufficient to go out into the air and open one's eyes to see that the world is not governed altogether by mechanism . . . When we gaze upon the multifariousness of nature we are looking straight into the face of living spontaneity."[81] Indeed, Peirce's rejection of materialism and his corresponding insistence on the reality of lived qualitative richness account for his seemingly idealist metaphysical assertions that quality is a "sleeping consciousness"[82] and that "it is a psychic feeling of red without us which arouses a sympathetic feeling of red in our senses"[83] Peirce is here objecting to the mechanistic view that barren primary qualities cause "less real" secondary qualities.

In light of the above analysis, three points can be noted, each of which will become relevant shortly. The first concerns the interrelation of the categories. According to Peirce, materialism, by omitting final causation, ignores Thirdness and, in so doing, omits spontaneity or, as he calls it in his cosmology, "objective chance," which belongs to the category of Firstness. The second point concerns the role of commonsense experience in understanding the nature of the metaphysically real. Commonsense experience is not to be ruled out as mere appearance in an attempt to grasp some ultimate metaphysical explanatory principle; instead, it is the key to understanding the nature of reality.[84] Third, though Peirce's cosmological account has been termed "the black sheep or the white elephant of his philosophical progeny,"[85] yet it is highly significant for understanding the interrelation of the categories as ontological, for it is Peirce's cosmology that in fact gives the "reason" for law.

After rejecting neutralism and materialism, Peirce accepts the only remaining alternative, idealism. What does this mean for Peirce at this point? It means that experience cannot be accounted for solely by mechanistic laws, which leave no place for chance, and that there is something more to nature than brute stupid action and reaction. It means that laws must be accounted for in terms of the process of cosmic evolution and that the richness of lived experience must find its place within the metaphysically real. It means that no part of the universe in its real concreteness is totally characterized either by the law of mind or the law of matter; that mind cannot be completely separated out from the activities of nature as a distinct mode of being, nor can the activities of nature be conflated to the activities of mind.

A reflection on those characteristics that Peirce is concerned to attribute to the universe seems to indicate that he is headed toward a temporalistic, pluralistic "idealism" without a block universe. It is an "idealism" that holds the law of mind to be in some yet-undetermined sense more fundamental than the law of matter but one that, nonetheless, views humans and their higher faculties as quite unessential to the processes of the universe. In short, Peirce here seems heading toward a naturalism that reintegrates humans and nature, not by reducing the human (as does the materialist), nor by assimilating nature to mind (as does the idealist), but by presenting an enriched nature within which are to be found the operations of those processes with which human activity is continuous.

Peirce, in his search for a metaphysical label, is here caught in what might be called the "Cartesian trap." If not dualism, then either all becomes mind or all becomes matter in the mechanistic sense of the nature or external world that remains when one cuts off the mind half of the Cartesian offering. What Peirce does not recognize in his survey of the traditional alternatives is that he has gone the path of those truly great philosophers who do not just take different alternatives among old choices but provide frameworks that reject the logic of the original questioning in terms of which both the problem and all its possible alternatives arise.

Peirce's difficulty in stating his position in any terms that will not be misunderstood can be seen from a statement that is probably aimed at dualism. He notes that

> Antisynechistic thinkers wind themselves up in a fictitious snarl by falsifying the phenomena in representing consciousness to be, as it were, a skin, a separate tissue, overlying an unconscious region of the occult nature, mind, soul, or physiological basis. It appears to me that in the present state of our knowledge a sound methodeutic prescribes that, in adhesion to the appearances, the difference is only relative and the demarcation not precise.[86]

Holmes, pouncing upon this remark, emphasizes Peirce's "behaviorism."[87] Peirce here is caught in a dilemma, for in attempting to avoid dualism, his terminology is caught between the horns of materialism and behaviorism on the one hand and idealism on the other. What he does not clearly see, and does not have adequate language to express, is that he has not asked the kind of question for which these alternatives can provide a satisfactory answer. He has asked a question concerning the behavior of the universe, and, believing that final causation is fundamental, he finds the only available conclusion to be that "The one intelligible theory of the universe is that of objective idealism, that matter is effete mind, inveterate habits becoming physical laws."[88] His understanding of the temporal process that constitutes the behavior of the universe likewise leads him to his idealistic claims, for "one of the most marked features about the law of mind [as opposed to the law of physical force] is that it makes time to have a definite direction of flow from past to future."[89] Indeed, investigation "must begin by asking what the flow of time consists in."[90]

However, no sooner does Peirce embrace idealism as the lesser of the available evils than he attempts to qualify his acceptance, for "The truth is that pragmaticism is closely allied to the Hegelian absolute idealism, from which, however, it is sundered by its vigorous denial that the third category . . . suffices to make the world, or is even so much as self-sufficient."[91] Peirce thus embraces objective idealism with reservations that lead to his assertion that his position is that of "conditional idealism."[92] Idealists, according to Peirce, have been correct in embracing the doctrine of final causation but, in understanding its nature, have endowed it with force or Secondness, which leaves no room for chance. Thus, we see that chance, or Firstness, requires not only Thirdness but also Secondness. Again, this clue to the interrelation of the categories must be put aside till later. Equally important, Peirce here does something seldom found in his writings. He here explicitly uses pragmatism, or pragmaticism, not as a theory of meaning, not as a theory of truth, not as a methodological principle, but as a metaphysical position, as a positive source for a distinct explanation of and orientation toward the nature of metaphysical reality. It is precisely the implications of this thin but pervasive thread of thought that this chapter hopes to lay bare. First, however, it is necessary to turn to Peirce's self-proclaimed scholastic realism.

In the above discussion the issue has been stated in terms of materialism, dualism, and idealism. It is within the context of these alternatives that Peirce was driven to an idealism modified by the insertion of the category of Secondness—and, indirectly, Firstness as well. This, however, leads directly to his realism, for though efficient causation belongs to the category of Secondness, the final causation indicated by Peirce's idealism belongs to the category of Thirdness, and it is with the reality of Thirdness that Peirce's realism is concerned. Furthermore, it will be seen that though Peirce's realism is concerned with the reality of Thirdness, the nature of Thirdness requires the reality of Secondness—and indirectly, Firstness as well.

That Peirce's realism is a crucial element in his philosophy is undeniable. However, as Boler has noted, though Peirce said he was a realist and though he said his realism was an important aspect of his philosophy, "it has been maintained, and with some justice, that it is impossible to find a clear statement of that realism in his writings."[93] In short, certain of Peirce's doctrines that he holds to be realistic are crucial to his philosophy. What must be determined is what is intended by these doctrines and whether this intended meaning can be adequately understood within the framework of the scholastic realism with which he identifies.

Peirce states the issue of realism in an apparently straightforward way: "Whether laws and general types are figments of the mind or are real."[94] That Peirce intends more by realism than is indicated by this seemingly straightforward question will become evident from his discussion of realism and from his objections to nominalism. Indeed, it is his objection to nominalism which gives the first glimmerings of the complexity of his realism. Peirce asserts that "all modern philosophy has been nominalistic."[95] This includes not only Locke, Berkeley, and Hume, but Leibniz and Hegel as well. Since Peirce criticized Hegelian idealism because it emphasized Thirdness, or "laws and general types," to the exclusiveness of Secondness, Peirce's realism cannot be understood merely by saying that Thirdness is real. It would seem at this point that realism in Peirce's view in some way involves Secondness. Yet, when we turn to Peirce's own often asserted affinity with the scholastic realism of Duns Scotus, it seems that it is the stance concerning the interrelationship of Secondness and Thirdness to which he objects. As he observes, "Even Duns Scotus is too nominalistic when he says that universals are contracted to the mode of individuality in singulars, meaning as he does, by singulars, ordinary existing things."[96]

The intimate interrelation of Secondness and Thirdness for Peirce is indicated to some extent in his statement that

> The court cannot be imagined without a sheriff. Final causality cannot be imagined without efficient causality; but no whit the

> less on that account are their modes of action polar contraries. The sheriff would still have his fist, even if there were no court; but an efficient cause, detached from a final cause in the form of a law would not even possess efficiency; it might exert itself, and something might follow post hoc, but not propter hoc; for propter implies potential regularity. Now without law there is no regularity; and without the influence of ideas there is no potentiality.[97]

Elsewhere Peirce writes that the court, or the category of Thirdness, "can have no concrete being without action, as a separate object on which to work its government."[98] Thus, it can be seen that efficient causation, in the sense of actualization of a possibility, requires the rational or "ideal causality"[99] of Thirdness to provide the potentialities, while Thirdness, apart from its concretion in Secondness, is not real. This leads Boler to say that there is a confusion in Peirce's position because of the "ambivalent role of Secondness. On the one hand, Secondness is the antigeneral, the brute, blind, and unintelligible—characterizations that are all negative or privative. On the other hand, Secondness is the actual without which laws and types cannot be real."[100] According to Boler, this confusion in Secondness leads indirectly to the problem of concretion, for Thirdness is not real without Secondness; yet, as Boler continues, Peirce holds that "secondness does not contain any thirdness at all. We have seen the same answer in another form: 'the would-be is never contracted to the is.'"[101] Thus, Secondness is bare or privative, Secondness does not contain any Thirdness, yet Thirdness is not real without Secondness. Boler concludes that Peirce has avoided the Scotistic theory that the real general is contracted in the individual by robbing existence of its richness and by replacing the mysterious notion of contraction with an equally mysterious notion of concretion through which the general becomes concrete in a world of actuality.

What accounts for this problem? Boler suggests that where Peirce's attack on the nominalist takes place within the context of a scholastic realism, his positive account of the status of laws and their relation to individuals occurs in the context of idealism. Boler observes that a thoroughgoing study of Peirce's idealism might shed some light on what he would say concerning the problems of concretion and of the barrenness of existence.[102] Thus, we are taken full circle back to the puzzles of Peirce's idealism.

If the "concrete being" of Thirdness as dependent upon Secondness is approached in the light of the traditional problems of contraction or concretion or ingression of any sort, Peirce's position may well be untenable. However, since once again Peirce is trying to deal with his position in terms of traditional alternatives, this time realism or nominalism, it may be that here again what underlies his difficulty in the search for an accurate label is a radical change in perspective such that the entire framework within which these traditional alternatives arise is rejected.

If Thirdness and Secondness are intimately interrelated, if Thirdness cannot be "imagined" without Secondness—yet Thirdness does not contract into Secondness—then another mode of interrelation is obviously called for. And, since it is Peirce's cosmological account, which, we have seen, gives the "reason" for law, a reason he thinks required by any adequate explanation, Peirce's cosmology may well hold the key to the ontological relation between Thirdness and Secondness. As will be indicated below, Peirce's cosmological account, in which the random actions and reactions of the substratum of pure chance gradually tend to take on habits which in turn limit future interactions, indicates a relation not of contraction but of emergence.

It may be held that to view the ontological problem of the relationship of the categories in terms of the cosmological problem of the origin of the categories is to commit a sort of genetic fallacy at the metaphysical level. However, only if the emergence of Thirdness from Secondness and Firstness is recognized can the status of Thirdness be adequately understood. Furthermore, as Goudge has pointed out, the sequence to be traced is not, in the initial stages, a temporal one at all. It is an objective logical sequence.[103] And only in the light of Peirce's cosmological account can one understand the sense in which it can be said that actuality can carry only a limited portion of possibility at any time, that the possibility of Thirdness is real only as it is in some sense "concrete in" the actual, and yet that Secondness does not "contain" any Thirdness at all.

Gallie, in discussing Peirce's cosmology, holds that "The fact is that, despite Peirce's efforts to show that such a primordial state would contain 'the germ of a generalizing tendency,' his accounts of it inevitably suggest a 'cosmic representation' of his First category alone; that is to say, he is supposing a state of affairs in which neither his Second nor his Third category would be manifested at all."[104] This criticism of Peirce perhaps holds the unrecognized key to understanding the relation of the categories, for what will be held below is that though the "primordial state" does suggest a "cosmic representation of the First category alone," this primordial state nonetheless contains the "germ of a generalizing tendency,"for the "germ" lies in Peirce's first category in the form of the degenerate generality or degenerate continuity of Firstness as a qualitative continuum.

As seen earlier, Peirce holds that Firstness is a negative generality or negative continuity, in that it does not limit the future as does law.[105] Firstness is also a pure possibility in relation to Secondness, for its being as possibility is not dependent upon its actualization.[106] From the indeterminate qualitative continuum,[107] which is logically prior to both Secondness and Thirdness, anything can occur, in that any two parts can interact. These random reactions occur from the brute, blind force of Secondness or efficient causation acting on the substratum of pure spontaneity. Firstness alone is a continuum of qualities, but, as seen earlier, "Firstness is essentially indifferent to continuity."[108] Yet though Firstness is essentially indifferent to its continuity, when interaction of two parts of the continuum occurs, that which interacts is continuous and provides a positive possibility of future interactions by excluding certain possibilities in its very occurrence. As Peirce indicates:

> Let the clean blackboard be a sort of diagram of the original vague potentiality . . . I draw a chalk line on the board. This discontinuity is one of these brute acts by which alone the original vagueness could have made a step toward definiteness. There is a certain element of continuity in this line. Where did this continuity come from? It is nothing but the original continuity of the blackboard which makes everything upon it continuous.[109]

Again, as Peirce notes, the discontinuity can be produced upon that blackboard only by the reaction between two continuous surfaces into which it is separated. Thus, what is a singularity or discreteness in the containing continuum is itself a positive generality in relation to the discrete cuts potentially "in" it. Charles Hartshorne has noted that "Continuity is the order of what can happen, not what does happen. . . . If continuity is the order of possibility it cannot be the order of actuality."[110] What the above discussion indicates, however, is that Hartshorne's formulation of the problem introduces a false dichotomy into the situation, for the chalk line can be viewed as discrete or continuous, as present actuality or present possibilities, depending upon whether one views the line as a cut in the containing continuum or as a continuous line determining the possibilities of future cuts within itself. In brief, Secondness, or bare brute action and reaction is a distinct analytic element within the ongoing process or evolving qualitative continuum. However, there is no such thing as disembodied interaction, and actuality as it contextually occurs in the passing present is characterized by the brute hereness and nowness of the shock of interaction or efficient causation "acting upon" the substratum of pure chance or "negative continuity" in accordance with the limitations placed upon it by the positive possibilities of Thirdness. Thus, though Peirce characterizes the individual as determinate in all respects, he notes, after delineating the category of Secondness in terms of the individual, that the absolute individual "cannot exist, properly speaking. For whatever lasts for any time, however short . . . will undergo some change in its relations."[111] In short, Secondness must provide the tool for progressing from the "may-be" or spontaneity of Firstness to the "would-be" or potentiality of Thirdness. In this sense, "Existence cannot transcend possibility. Whatever exists is possible. But it is impossible that all possibilities should exist."[112]

Here it may be objected that there is a sense in which the cuts do contain the continuum, for it was stated that the possibilities inherent in the continuum cut are partially dependent upon the possibilities inherent in the continuum from which it is cut. However, this latter relationship is not admissible as indicative of a relationship between Thirdness and Secondness, for it depends upon viewing the cut, not in its aspect of discreteness or Secondness, but in its aspect of continuity or Thirdness. Thus Peirce can hold that final causality is operative in nature and that things tend toward a final cause. Present processes tend to realize a future that is inherent within them as present possibilities. As Peirce observes, "Final causation is that kind of causation whereby the whole calls out its parts."[113] This whole is not some idealistic type of "ens necessarium" that "draws" the processes of nature, nor is it any "whole of nature" trying to realize itself; rather, the whole is any continuum of natural processes that "calls out" a determinate range of parts. The rationality of final causality is the rational force of continuity. To say that processes are governed by final causes is to say that potentialities are real, for final causes within nature are continuities that govern their possible cuts or actualities, but that no number of actualities can exhaust.

Thus, acts or Secondness can be characterized both as privative, brute, blind or unintelligible and as that which gives reality to laws and general types. Secondness, as distinct from Firstness or Thirdness, is a brute action and reaction. In this sense it is the acting compulsion of efficient causation. Secondness is a mode of behavior of the concrete qualitative continuum—the mode of behavior that is characterized by efficient causation. It is the bruteness of interaction of two parts of a qualitative process. Existence, then, is a mode of behavior of the general; it is the mode of behavior characterized by interaction. And, it is the interaction, not that which interacts, that is individual, brute, and blind. But this brute, blind interaction of the general qualitative continuum is what turns negative possibility into positive possibility, mere may-be into would-be. Thus, Secondness is that which makes possible the very reality of Thirdness.

It can be seen, then, why Peirce insists that Thirdness does not contract into Secondness: Thirdness is not the kind of "thing" that can be in Secondness. Indeed, if one insists on using spatial language, it is more accurate to say that Secondness is in Thirdness than that Thirdness is in Secondness, for a continuum may be said to contain its cuts, potential or actual, but the cuts do not contain the continuum.[114] Thus, Peirce can say that Secondness does not contain any Thirdness at all, for an "*existing* thing is simply a blind reacting thing," though "existing *things* do not need supporting reasons; for they are reasons."[115] Here can be found the radical significance of Peirce's view that synechism and realism are intimately linked.[116]

As developed above, actuality can carry only a limited portion of possibilities, yet positive possibilities are real only as they are "concrete in" the actual. The analogy of the chalk line brought the meaning of this statement into focus, for the actuality of the chalk line was an actualization of one of many possibilities inherent in the containing continuum. Yet, the chalk line, in its aspect of continuity, contains positive possibilities of future cuts, and the character of these positive possibilities is dependent upon the character of the containing continuum from which it has risen. Thus, it becomes clear that the emergence of Thirdness from Secondness and Firstness does not mean that a continuum can emerge from a series of discrete cuts, but that Secondness provides the tool for progressing from the negative continuity of Firstness to the positive continuity of Thirdness. As such, the present is rich both in quality and potentiality.[117]

It may seem that the above analysis of the interrelation of Peirce's categories is itself peculiarly lacking in broad temporal reference. However, the relation between actuality and possibility within the passing present indirectly indicates the way in which the past and future relate to the present. The ensuing discussion will turn more explicitly to this temporal focus.

Peirce's philosophy is at times accused of an "over-futurism." And, indeed, Peirce does claim that reality consists in the future.[118] However, this is not a metaphysical statement but an epistemological claim.[119] Successful prediction is the only way we can know that our meaningful claims fall within the range of alternatives presented by the tendencies in nature. Yet, even when clearly distinguished from epistemological issues, his metaphysics is nonetheless at times accused of over-futurism, for it is held that the emphasis on the would-be of real potentialities requires that the future actuality be real now in some sense. This type of accusation, however, evinces a confusion concerning the temporal significance of the categorial interrelation that Peirce provides. There is a very great difference among "future actualizations," "future possibilities of actualizations," and "present possibilities of future actualizations," though these (and especially the second and third) are often used interchangeably. The difference between possibility and actuality is not the difference between future and present; instead, past, present, and future can be viewed in terms of possibility or actuality. When these various facets are distinguished, it becomes evident that Peirce's emphasis on the would-be does not put undue emphasis on the future and does not require that future actualizations in some sense be real now; rather, it requires that *present possibilities for* future actualization be real.

If only past and future actuality were involved, then the passing present would be merely a deterministic push from the past or pull from the future. However, past and future are conditions involved in the present, not in their aspect of actuality, but in their aspect of continuity or possibility. Furthermore, even in their aspect of possibility, the past and the future do not denote settled entities that have been or will be, for just as past and future enter into the total character of the passing present, actuality enters into the character of the past and the future, changing the possibilities inherent in them as real possibilities. Future as well as past are drawn into the present for Peirce, but they are drawn into the present in the form of potentialities and possibilities engaged in an ever-advancing process of actualization. This is possible only because the present contains actualizations, potentialities and possibilities, all emergent from the past and projecting toward a novel future.

Once again, Peirce's analogy of the chalk line may be helpful. The past actualizing of a first chalk line has an aspect of continuity which contains possibilities present now in a second chalk line, cut somewhere across the containing one. Yet, the second chalk line, as an actualizing event in the emerging present, has eliminated forever certain possibilities that before were real possibilities. They are no longer pasts for a next emerging chalk line. Further, the present chalk line is "rich with the future" because of the real present possibilities of future cuts that reflect upon its character; indeed, its character can be said to be constituted by those present possibilities. Thus, the unique, unpredictable hereness and nowness of present actuality changes the character of the past as it pushes into the future, but it can do this only because it is continuous with and partially determined by the past and the future in the sense indicated above. It can be seen, then, that Peirce puts undue emphasis neither on the future nor on the past; he draws the past and the future into the present in the form of present possibilities which are real now, though not actual.

The above sketch gives some indication of the way the interaction of the categories of Secondness and Thirdness yields a position that escapes the Scotistic notion of contraction of a real common object without winding up in the idealist problem of concretion and without negating the richness of temporal existence. Furthermore, it paves the way for a further integration of Peirce's diverse characterizations and uses of ontological Firstness.

Observing the fact that both "abstract qualities" and "chance variations" belong to the category of Firstness, Douglas Greenlee states that they seem to have in common only the fact that they are neither Seconds nor Thirds and therefore are relegated to the category of Firsts. In light of this he notes that it may well be asked why chance variations should not be assigned to some new fourth category.[120] On this view, Firstness seems to have become the systematic dump-heap for that which will not fit into the categories of Secondness or Thirdness. Yet, if Firstness is indeed first, one would expect it to provide the significant starting point for the metaphysical functions assigned to the other categories. If, as here held, qualitative richness and chance variation are intimately interrelated as together forming the nature of the primordial substratum, then the need for some "new fourth category" dissolves, and Firstness does indeed become the significant starting point of Peirce's metaphysics, for it indicates the infinitely varied, concrete qualitative richness "felt"[121] in experience, the substratum of pure chance within which random activities occur and give rise to emergent habit-takings. This dual role of Firstness can help clarify the meaning of Peirce's claim, often viewed as supportive of his self-proclaimed idealism, that "Wherever chance-spontaneity is found, there in the same proportion feeling exists. In fact, chance is but the outward aspect of that which within itself is feeling."[122]

The above analysis of the interrelation of the categories leads back to the problem of understanding Peirce's proclamation of idealism on the basis of a belief that the "law of mind" is more fundamental than the "law of matter," for on the above interpretation of Peirce's transformation of scholastic realism it would seem that Secondness or efficient causation or the "law of matter" is logically prior to Thirdness or final causation or the "law of mind." Here it is important to stress the distinction between the mechanistic materialism against which Peirce was reacting and his own view as to those qualities that best characterize "matter" as opposed to "mind," a distinction that at times shows itself clearly in his writings, yet at times seems almost not to exist.

It has already been seen that the difference between the physical and the mental cannot be represented in Peirce's philosophy as differences inside the substantive framework of the categories of "thing" of "stuff." What has not yet been clearly pointed out is that Peirce gives his own positive characterization of matter not in terms of efficient causation as opposed to final causation but in terms of the rigidity of fixed habit versus the spontaneity of habit taking. It will be remembered that Peirce's choice of idealism as the "one intelligible theory of the universe" is stated in the view that "matter is effete mind, inveterate habits becoming physical laws."

To say the law of mind is prior to the law of matter is not to say final causation is prior to efficient causation but rather to say spontaneity is prior to regularity. As Peirce states, "Uncertain tendencies, unstable states of equilibrium are conditions sine qua non for the manifestation of mind,"[123] while matter is "mind whose habits have become fixed so as to lose the powers of forming them and losing them."[124] Again, "All phenomena are of one character, though some are more mental and spontaneous, others more material and regular. Still all alike present that mixture of freedom and constraint which allows them to be, nay, makes them to be teleological, or purposive."[125]

The freedom and constraint displayed by "all phenomena" are "there" in the qualitative continuum, the substratum of chance. The freedom lies in the potential for chance interactions or cuts within the containing continuum. The constraint lies in the nature of the substratum as the negative continuity or negative generality of the may-be that random reactions turn into positive potentialities that limit possible future interactions. The spontaneity is a spontaneity for new habit-takings, for emerging new centers of positive potentialities within the containing general continuum. The difficulty of separating the aspects of efficient and final causation, of brute interaction and continuity or lawfulness, even for purposes of analysis, is laid bare in Peirce's observation that "In one aspect of the matter it would be perfectly true to say that final causation is alone primary." But on the other hand, the law of habit is "a law of efficient causation; so that either way of regarding the matter is equally true, although the former is more intelligent."[126]

The above discussion has focused on chance or spontaneity as belonging to the category of Firstness, and thus it may seem that Firstness alone houses the element of emergence or creativity. This error can best be brought to light by way of an interesting thesis by Carl Hausman,[127] which holds that Peirce's concern with the origin and aim of the evolutionary process requires the notion of agape as an addition to his three fundamental categories in order to account for creative growth, which includes "radical creativity."[128] According to this thesis, Peirce's account requires more than a category of spontaneity, it requires agape, as the principle of permissive love. The ensuing discussion will pursue certain insights in that essay to clarify the concept of creativity implicit in Peirce's pragmatic metaphysics as developed above. It will agree with Hausman's position in holding that Peirce's understanding of creativity, or in the present context, creative emergence, cannot be adequately grasped through one of Peirce's three general categories. Rather than turning to the principle of agape, however, it will claim that emergence or creativity is itself an emergent feature of the interrelation of the three Peircean categories.

Firstness includes negative possibility, pure diversity, temporally grounded negative continuity. As such it is a substratum of pure chance. However, this does not adequately capture the role of chance, for, as Peirce indicates, "I make use of chance chiefly to make room for a principle of generalization, or tendency to form habits, which I hold has produced all regularities."[129] Again, he speaks of "chance in the form of a spontaneity which is to some degree regular."[130] What the above discussion indicates is that although the key to understanding creativity or emergence is Peirce's category of Firstness, this type of novelty cannot be identified merely with the chance spontaneity of the category of Firstness. There is, as Hausman again so well expresses, "the integration of telos and spontaneity in creativity."[131] In describing Peirce's position, William James observes that to an observer standing outside of its generating conditions, "novelty can appear only as so much 'chance,' while to one who stands inside it is the expression of 'free creative activity.'"[132] Free creative activity, as opposed to the compulsion of blind spontaneous chance, requires the positive continuity or telos of Thirdness as well as the Secondness which brings such telos into being. This is perhaps analogous to Peirce's view that Secondness "is act, not power,"[133] for power requires the interrelation of all three categories.

Cosmic creativity, then, can be understood only in terms of all three of the Peircean categories. Firstness, as the negative possibility or substratum of chance, is the substratum for alternative realizations of potentialities. Secondness, as brute action and reaction, as the idealized limiting point of the temporal moment, is the idealized moment productive of interactive novelty. Thirdness or potentiality or lawfulness, as the would-be that, in coming to be, changes the range of real possibilities "there" for its further development, is at once the foundation of lawful endurance and the bearer of a novel future. This categorial interrelationship displays the key feature that for Hausman calls for agape: a process that progresses toward new intelligibility; a process in which the telos of the process itself changes, rather than a process that conforms to a predetermined telos that prestructures it.[134] Thus, while cosmic creativity is not reducible to the category of chance spontaneity, neither does it require a principle of agape in addition to the interrelation of the three categories. Instead, cosmic creativity, as free creative activity, as emergence, arises within the dynamic interrelation of the three Peircean categories.[135] Human creativity, which has been seen to be evinced in abductive activity, in the play of imagination, in metaphor, and in fact to permeate all levels of epistemic activity, can be understood as a uniquely specialized, highly intensified instance of the free creative activity characteristic of the universe within which it functions,[136] and the conditions of possibility of human freedom in general, as self-directedness rooted in rationality,[137] are to be found in the conditions that constitute the universe at large and within which rationality emerges.[138]

It can be seen, then, that Peirce's self-proclaimed idealism and realism, when viewed within the context of the many, at times perplexing and seemingly contradictory, qualifications that he makes, become interwoven with that thin but pervasive thread of pragmatic metaphysical doctrine to produce the strong textures of a pragmatic metaphysics of action that undercuts the alternatives offered by a tradition of substance metaphysics.[139] It has been seen that this reality Peirce envisions is characterized not by discrete things or repeatable universals but by a concrete continuum inexhaustibly rich in possibilities and potentialities. It "swims in indeterminacy"[140] precisely because of its inexhaustible richness. This pragmatic metaphysics of activity indicates that while reality grounds our beliefs, it cannot provide the basis for an ideally true and final opinion or support convergence toward final knowledge. Rather, Peirce's metaphysics, in conjunction with his epistemology, provides the solid philosophical underpinnings for the worldly pluralism of a Kuhnsian-Peircean interpretation of science as presented at the start of this work.

An examination of these underpinnings has revealed that at all levels of awareness human creative noetic activity enters into what is grasped, and different ways of grasping, governed by different habits of response or rule guided activity, will yield different contents grasped. Facts, and indeed the very conceivability of what facts there can be, emerge from the backdrop of world as an unthematic perspective or "outermost" horizon of meaningful rapport with the independently real. And, even within a commonly held commonsense world, different abstract articulations, different abstract worlds, will give rise to different theoretical facts. Further, the most immediately apprehended sense contents or "appearances" that serve as verification instances in experience are partially structured by the facts that we expect them to represent, for they emerge in experience as perspectives of objects through the functioning of habit as generative of schematic aspects. Indeed, even the sensory core of the schemata that help structure these appearances is not pure datum but partially the product of the synthesizing activity of mind.

It has been seen that Peirce's claims of realism as opposed to nominalism, far from exceeding the bounds of his pragmatic theory of meaning, are virtually demanded by it. Further, his "proofs" of realism reveal that while lawfulness runs throughout experience, the manner in which the abundance of such modes of behavior is made intelligible is itself partially dependent upon the perspectival approach of noetic creativity.

It has been seen also that Peirce, in his drive toward metaphysics, utilizes a phenomenology of experience that is itself experimental, fallible, and ultimately pluralistic in method, yielding metaphysical categories the nature of which reflect these features. And the metaphysical categories that emerge through this endeavor yield an understanding of nature or the dynamical object which, as an indefinitely rich evolving continuum that must be made determinate for our awareness by the manner in which we "cut" into it, cannot provide the basis for final ultimate knowledge. Nature or the dynamical object, with its qualitative richness, lawful modes of behavior, and emerging activities, constrains our interpretations, pulling them or coaxing them in some directions rather than others. It answers our questions and determines the workability of our meaning structures, but what answers it gives are partially dependent on what questions we ask, and what meaning structures work are partially dependent upon the structures we bring. Thus, within this interactive context of interpretation and constraint, different structurings yield different isolatable dynamical objects, different things, different facts. Truth is always related to a context of interpretation. This is not because truth is relative but because without a context of interpretation the concept of truth is senseless, indeed literally so. Knowledge involves convergence, but convergence within a common world that we have partially made, and continually remake in various of its aspects and in various ways.

Within this interactive context of creativity and constraint, it has been seen that traditional alternatives fall by the wayside. Neither reality nor the relation of thought to reality can be characterized in terms of the alternatives of traditional realism, idealism, or phenomenalism. Truth can be understood neither as coherence nor as correspondence. Knowledge, and human awareness in general, can be characterized neither as foundationalist nor as antifoundationalist. And, finally, pragmatic pluralism, as the alternative to convergence toward a final ultimate opinion, cannot be understood in terms of relativism, subjectivism, or irrational arbitrariness as opposed to "objectivism" and rational progress. Peirce's entire orientation provides a novel paradigm in which these popular but self-defeating dichotomies become irrelevant. This new paradigm provides the context for an enriching philosophical kinship between Peirce and Kuhn, showing that Kuhn's understanding of the pluralistic nature of scientific change does not render such change arbitrary or irrational, nor does Peirce's understanding of scientific progress render such progress at odds with inherent pluralism.

In conclusion, there should perhaps be a retrospective view of a point made in the introduction. It was there noted that the intent of the present work is not to provide some sort of refutation of more traditional interpretations of Peirce's writings but to offer an alternative perspective that highlights and interrelates the pragmatic, systematic, and pluralistic dimensions of his thought in a new and hopefully fruitful way. If this attempt has been at all successful, what it perhaps shows is that the richness of Peirce's writings, like the richness of the reality he presents, cannot totally prestructure the intelligibilities to which it gives rise.

ENDNOTES

INTRODUCTION

1. *Collected Papers of Charles Sanders Peirce,* vols. 1–6, ed. Charles Hartshorne and Paul Weiss (Cambridge: Belknap Press of Harvard University, 1931–35); vols. 7–8, ed. Arthur Burks (Cambridge: Harvard University Press, 1958), 8.262. (Henceforth cited as *CP* and using conventional two-part notation.) This statement is made in the context of his support of theism over positions which imply polytheism, but the discussion far transcends this limited issue.

2. Ibid.

3. This is a key issue in the discussion between H. S. Thayer and some of his critics in "Perspectives on the History of Pragmatism: A Symposium on H. S. Thayer's Meaning and Action: A Critical History of Pragmatism," *Transactions of the Charles S. Peirce Society: A Quarterly Journal in American Philosophy* 11 (1975): 229–88, esp. 237, 240, 263–64, 275–78.

1. WORLD, TRUTH, AND SCIENCE

1. Thomas Kuhn, *The Structure of Scientific Revolutions,* 2d ed. (Chicago: The University of Chicago Press, 1970), p. 126. Emphasis added.

2. There is implied here a rejection of ontological phenomenalism. The issue of ontological phenomenalism concerns the objective reference of the contents of awareness. Ontological phenomenalism holds that the contents of awareness—at whatever level of complexity they are grasped—are either the only reality there is or the only reality that can be known, rather than a grasp of a "hard," external, independent reality.

3. This implies a rejection of idealism.

4. Thus, realism is here denied. The precise nature of the realism being denied will be clarified later in the chapter.

5. This point is discussed in some historical detail by C. I. Lewis in relation to the development of his own position. See *Mind and the World Order* (New York: Dover, 1929), 154. Although Kant is consid-

ered to begin "the rejection of the spectator," he himself was not immune to some of its presuppositions. Thus, in accepting the later two characteristics, he rejected the first.

6. *CP* 3.527.

7. *CP* 8.148.

8. *CP* 2.143. Of course there is a sense in which other "worlds" are real. For example, the ideal world is a real ideal world.

9. *CP* 2.141.

10. *CP* 3.529.

11. *CP* 3.527.

12. Ibid.

13. Ibid.

14. It is not necessary here to distinguish between metaphysical possibility as the "may-be" of Firstness and as the "would-be" of Thirdness, a distinction that will prove crucial in chapter 5. What is important here is the distinction between metaphysical possibility of any type and the epistemic possibilities contained within our meaning structures.

15. *CP* 4.67, 3.527.

16. *CP* 3.527.

17. *CP* 3.527.

18. *CP* 3.531.

19. *CP* 4.67.

20. *CP* 4.68.

21. *CP* 3.527.

22. *CP* 1.171–72. This claim will be developed in depth in chapter 5.

23. *CP* 1.171. Peirce argues here that all things swim, like fallibilistic knowledge, in continua of indeterminacy.

24. Peirce asserts that the general is that to which the law of the excluded middle does not apply, while the vague is that to which the principle of noncontradiction does not apply (*CP* 5.448). He then explicitly identifies continuity with generality (*CP* 8.279; *The Microfilm Edition of the Peirce Papers,* Houghton Library, Harvard University, MS 137, pp. 7–12 [Henceforth identified by manuscript and page numbers only].) And, for Peirce, whatever is general or continuous is to some degree vague. Thus, neither the law of noncontradiction nor the law of excluded middle is perfectly applicable to the continuous. (This point will be introduced again in chapter 5.)

25. *CP* 2.34. Though Peirce is referring to Hegel's method in the long discussion in which this statement is housed, this particular statement refers to Peirce's own modification, as can be seen by the context and by references given there to other of his claims.

26. Here it must be stressed that what is ontologically possible

cannot be defined as that which obeys the law of noncontradiction, for as indicated above, the law of noncontradiction applies to our conceptual structures and that which is grasped by them, not to the continuous processes of nature that are given for conceptual interpretation.

27. MS 647, p. 8.

28. *CP* 3.420 n. 1.

29. *CP* 6.67. For an analysis of Peirce's attack on Mill concerning different points and coming from a vastly different direction than that of the present work, see Richard Smyth, "Peirce's Examination of Mill's Philosophy," *Transactions of the Charles S. Peirce Society: A Quarterly Journal in American Philosophy* 21 (1985): 157–99.

30. *CP* 8.261. See also his claim, which will be utilized in the following chapter, that "There is no *thing* which is in itself in the sense of not being relative to the mind, though things which are relative to the mind doubtless *are,* apart from that relation" (*CP* 5.311).

31. MS 942, p. 16.

32. MS 642, p. 16.

33. MS 634, p. 9.

34. John Lachs, "Peirce, Santayana, and the Large Facts," *Transactions of the Charles S. Peirce Society: A Quarterly Journal in American Philosophy* 16 (1980): 12.

35. This Platonic line of interpretation is presented, for example, by W. P. Haas, *The Conception of Law and the Unity of Peirce's Philosophy* (Notre Dame: University of Notre Dame Press, 1964), 99, and will be discussed in more detail in chapter 5.

36. *CP* 3.527.

37. *CP* 6.200.

38. The relation of the internal structure of meaning to the structure of the diagrammatic nature of theorematic reasoning in mathematics will be developed in detail in chapter 2.

39. *CP* 2.302.

40. *CP* 2.228. Timothy Alborn claims that Peirce did take a Platonist turn but later "substituted semiotics for Platonism as the system holding together his continuous relational network" ("Peirce's Evolutionary Logic: Continuity, Indeterminacy, and the Natural Order," *Transactions of the Charles S. Peirce Society: A Quarterly Journal in American Philosophy* 25 1989: 6).

41. *CP* 1.209.

42. MS 427, pp. 40–41.

43. Robert Almeder, "Peirce's Thirteen Theories of Truth," *Transactions of the Charles S. Peirce Society: A Quarterly Journal in American Philosophy* 21 (1985): 91.

44. Robert Almeder, *The Philosophy of Charles S. Peirce* (New Jersey: Rowman and Littlefield, 1980), 52.

45. Joseph Esposito, *Evolutionary Metaphysics: The Development of Peirce's Theory of Categories* (Athens: Ohio University Press, 1980), 229.

46. Robert Almeder, "The Epistemological Realism of Charles Peirce," *Transactions of the Charles S. Peirce Society: A Quarterly Journal in American Philosophy* 11 (1975): pp. 3–17.

47. Ibid., 14 Emphasis added.

48. Ibid., 9 Emphasis added.

49. The idealism under discussion here is of course epistemological rather than metaphysical idealism, though the two are certainly not unrelated.

50. This is precisely the conclusion reached by Almeder. See "Fallibilism and the Ultimate Irreversible Opinion," *American Philosophical Quarterly Monograph* no. 9 (1975). John E. Smith refers to Peirce's theory of truth as a "conform" theory, which has a distinct advantage over the term *correspondence* in that it can avoid much of the historical baggage attaching to the term *correspondence,* but it operates nonetheless within a framework of realism and ultimate convergence (*Purpose and Thought: The Meaning of Pragmatism* [New Haven: Yale University Press], 50ff.).

51. Some type of coherence, theory of truth operates within the framework of ontological phenomenalism as well.

52. Perhaps the term *perspectival realism* seems appropriate at this point, and it may well be. Yet, this label does not seem to quite capture the full import or implications of Peirce's pragmatic theory of truth. For illuminating insights into issues of realism and truth see Carl Hausman's *Charles S. Peirce's Evolutionary Philosophy* (New York: Cambridge University Press, 1993) 208–15 passim.

53. MS 934, p. 24.

54. MS 647, p. 26.

55. MS 647, p. 9.

56. *CP* 5.565–68.

57. Ibid.

58. *CP* 5.566.

59. *CP* 5.565.

60. Ibid.

61. MS 409, p. 112.

62. Ibid.

63. Ibid.

64. *CP* 1.405.

65. *CP* 3.432. Emphasis in the original text.

66. *CP* 4.61.

67. H. S. Thayer, *Meaning and Action: A Critical History of Pragmatism* (Bobbs-Merrill Co.: Indianapolis and New York, 1968), 132. See also Murray Murphey, *The Development of Peirce's Philosophy* (Cambridge: Harvard University Press, 1961), 302.

68. MS 967, p. 1.

69. Helmut Pape, "Laws of Nature, Rules of Conduct and their Analogy in Peirce's Semiotics," *Transactions of the Charles S. Peirce Society: A Quarterly Journal in American Philosophy* 20 (1984): 220.

70. Robert Almeder, "Scientific Progress and Peircean Utopian Realism," *Erkenntnis* 20 (1983): 253–80.

71. Bruce Altuschuler, "Peirce's Theory of Truth and the Revolt Against Realism," *Transactions of the Charles S. Peirce Society: A Quarterly Journal in American Philosophy* 18 (1982): 34. C. F. Delaney, in *Science, Knowledge, and Mind: A Study in the Philosophy of C. S. Peirce* (Notre Dame and London: University of Notre Dame Press, 1993) also reads Peirce as a scientific realist. Unfortunately this book became available too late to be used as a focal point for the present discussion.

As seen earlier in this chapter, Peirce is a scientific realist of sorts. But this does not involve the "furniture" type of realism, nor does it involve the ontological privileging of science suggested by Peirce's interpreters quoted here.

72. *Writings of Charles S. Peirce: A Chronological Edition* (Bloomington: Indiana University Press, 1984), 1.496.

73. Hjalmar Wennerberg, *The Pragmatism of C. S. Peirce* (Lund: CWK Gleerup; Copenhagen: Ejnar Munksgaard, 1962), 147.

74. Peter Skagestad, *The Road of Inquiry: Charles Peirce's Pragmatic Realism* (New York: Columbia University Press, 1981), 127. Since Skagestad interprets Peirce as denying this distinction, he of course does not utilize it in any of his analyses of Peirce's position; this results in conflations of issues that could perhaps better be separated.

75. Ibid.

76. These points will all be developed in detail in the following chapter.

77. *CP* 2.302.

78. *CP* 8.191, 2.29.

79. *CP* 4.71.

80. *CP* 1.132.

81. *CP* 1.73.

82. *CP* 5.376, note 1 of second set of footnotes.

83. MS 290, pp. 2–3.

84. The importance of this point was brought home to me through

Vincent Colapietro's helpful comments concerning the paper I presented at the Charles S. Peirce Sesquicentennial International Congress, Harvard University, 1989.

85. *CP* 6.17, 1.105.

86. *CP* 6.58.

87. *CP* 6.109ff.

88. *CP* 1.109.

89. *CP* 5.509.

90. *CP* 4.235.

91. This point will be developed in the next chapter.

92. *CP* 5.522.

93. MS 427, p. 41.

94. MS 286, p. 1.

95. *CP* 4.237.

96. The direction for understanding, in a way compatible with the present interpretation, how a shared meaningfulness of incommensurable scientific worlds can be rooted in the commonalty of the relatively "acritically indubitable" but "invariably vague" commonsense world, but without falling into foundationalism, is indicated by T. L. Short, "Peirce and the Incommensurability of Theories," in *The Relevance of Charles Peirce,* ed. Eugene Freeman, The Monist Library of Philosophy, (La Salle, Ill.: Hegeler Institute, 1983), 119–31.

97. *CP* 2.753, 5.513. Christopher Hookway, taking a position contrary to the present view, seems to hold that the vague, indubitable commonsense beliefs will lead to convergence on theoretical matters (*Peirce,* [London: Routledge and Kegan Paul, 1985], 230).

98. *CP* 5.522.

99. It should be remembered that in denying scientific realism what is being denied is the "furniture realism" that allows for correspondence, here at the scientific level, and also the ontological privileging of the findings of science.

100. John McDermott notes that Peirce "early anticipated what we now take to be a truism: that the major problems which loom before us rarely will yield . . . even to the activity of a single method" (*Streams of Experience: Reflections on the History and Philosophy of American Culture* [Amherst: The University of Massachusetts Press, 1986], 101–2). Within the present context, this claim could be made about alternative particular methods and rules, though scientific method in the broad sense intended in Peirce's philosophy and explicated throughout this work is not one alternative method among others but *the* method of fixing belief.

101. *CP* 6.529ff., 6.476, 6.477, 7.220–21. Edward Madden insightfully points out that explanatory power cannot be reduced to predictive scope ("Discussing James and Peirce With Meyers," *Transactions of*

the Charles S. Peirce Society: A Quarterly Journal in American Philosophy 25 [1989]: 146).

102. Nicholas Rescher, *Peirce's Philosophy of Science* (Notre Dame: University of Notre Dame Press, 1978), 89–90.

103. *CP* 6.476.

104. *CP* 5.446.

105. Peirce, *Writings,* 4.545–46; *CP* 1.72ff., 2.780.

106. Skagestad, *Road of Inquiry,* 127.

107. Susan Haack, "Extreme Scholastic Realism: Its Relevance to Philosophy of Science Today," *Transactions of the Charles S. Peirce Society: A Quarterly Journal in American Philosophy* 28 (1992): 32, 35.

108. Rescher, *Peirce's Philosophy of Science,* 26–29.

109. *CP* 6.181.

110. Peirce, *Writings,* 1.489. Emphasis in the original text.

111. *CP* 5.265.

2. MEANING AS HABIT

1. Thomas Olshewsky, "A Third Dogma of Empiricism," *The Monist,* 49 (1965): 304–18.

2. Robert Almeder, "Peirce on Meaning," *Synthese* 41 (1979): 1–24.

3. Manley Thompson, "Peirce's Verificationist Realism," *The Review of Metaphysics* 23 (1978): 74–98.

4. Bruce Altuschuler, "The Nature of Peirce's Pragmatism," *Transactions of the Charles S. Peirce Society: A Quarterly Journal in American Philosophy* 14 (1978): 147–75.

5. Both of these issues will gain in significance in later chapters.

6. *CP* 1.443.

7. *CP* 1.248.

8. *CP* 1.633. What Peirce here means by "practical infallibility" is that one ought to obey the body of accepted beliefs and not one's own individual reason. Here there is no problem of doubt that is not real living doubt, although in another passage in which Peirce refers to the term (*CP* 7.108) there is such a problem.

9. *CP* 1.443.

10. *CP* 1.248.

11. *CP* 1.661.

12. *CP* 4.232.

13. Susan Haack, in "Fallibilism and Necessity" (*Synthese* 41 [1979]: 37–63), disagrees with the following interpretation, holding that the starting points of mathematics are themselves necessary.

14. *CP* 4.232.

15. *CP* 4.233.

16. *CP* 1.443.

17. Charles S. Peirce, *The New Elements of Mathematics,* ed. Carolyn Eisele (The Hague: Mouton Press, 1976), 4.49.

18. *CP* 2.778. Peirce here indicates clearly that "diagrammic" and "schematic" are to be used interchangeably.

19. *CP* 2.778.

20. Ibid.

21. *CP* 4.478.

22. *CP* 4.233.

23. Jaakko Hintikka, "C. S. Peirce's 'First Real Discovery' and Its Contemporary Relevance," *The Monist* 63 (1980).

24. Kenneth L. Ketner, "How Hintikka Misunderstood Peirce's Account of Theorematic Reasoning," *Transactions of the Charles S. Peirce Society: A Quarterly Journal in American Philosophy* 21 (1985).

25. Jerry Dozoretz, "The Internally Real, the Fictitious, and the Indubitable," in *Studies in Peirce's Semiotic,* ed. Kenneth Ketner and Joseph Ransdell (Lubbock, Tex.: Institute for Studies in Pragmatism, 1979), 82.

26. *CP* 4.233.

27. Ibid.

28. MS 1105, p. 4.

29. Peirce, *New Elements of Mathematics,* 4.21. It must be remembered that icons, as schemata, involve elements of Firstness, Secondness, and Thirdness, or image, activity, and rule.

30. MS 288, p. 95. In Hugh Joswick's discussion of the relation of theorematic reasoning to interpretation in general, the iconic nature of diagrammatic reasoning has been stressed, resulting in the conclusion that if we are to deduce more than is explicitly signified, we must resort to theorematic reasoning and replace the symbolic general sign by an icon, though we do not require the construction of diagrams in ordinary discourse ("Peirce's Mathematical Model of Interpretation," *Transactions of the Charles S. Peirce Society: A Quarterly Journal in American Philosophy* 24 [1988]). According to the present view, diagrammatic or schematic reasoning is involved in *all* thinking and perceptual awareness.

31. MS 293, p. 14.

32. *CP* 2.81.

33. Peirce of course does not accept Kant's absolute system of categories with their transcendental schemata, for experience is not limited by fixed modes of intuition and fixed forms of thought. Rather, all schemata are schemata of empirical concepts. For Peirce, the essential criteria for the application of a concept to experience are given in the

schemata. It should perhaps be clarified here that this chapter is not concerned with Peirce's own categories in relation to Kant.

34. See, for example, *CP* 5.491, 5.486.

35. This distinction refers to the epistemic and ontological dimensions of meaning in terms of habit. There is intended no reference here to "habit-takings" of the universe.

36. Almeder, "Epistemological Realism of Charles Peirce," 10–11.

37. In resolving the issue of phenomenalism there are two key questions, which can perhaps best be called, for purposes of distinction, the logical or epistemological question and the ontological question. The first concerns the level of complexity of that of which consciousness is aware: Do we build objectives out of more primitive contents of awareness, or is the perception of objectivity fundamental? The second question concerns the objective reference of the content of awareness: Are the contents of awareness—at whatever level of complexity—either the only reality there is or the only reality that can be known, or is the content of awareness a direct grasp (though not necessarily a "spectator" grasp) of a "hard," external, independent reality? An affirmative answer to the first alternative offered by either the epistemological question or the ontological question places one within the phenomenalist camp in some sense. The present chapter argues that Peirce accepts the second alternative offered by the epistemological question, thus indicating his rejection of this type of phenomenalism. The ontological issue will be discussed in later chapters.

38. *CP* 4.9.

39. *CP* 8.326, 8.332, 5.289. It must be emphasized that purposive biological activity, as the foundation of meaning, cannot be understood in terms of scientific contents. Rather, it is the "lived-through" biological activity of the human organism and, as such, is capable of phenomenological description and logical analysis. The dimensions of phenomenological description and logical analysis will both take on added significance later in this chapter.

40. *CP* 5.416, 5.213, 7.465.

41. *CP* 5.531.

42. Ibid

43. *CP* 5.298–99.

44. Peirce expresses his intent to "avoid all danger of being understood as attempting to explain a concept by percepts, images, schemata, or by anything but concepts," thereby denying that "acts, which are more strictly singular than anything, could constitute the purport, or adequate proper interpretation, of any symbol." As he continues, "no doubt, Pragmaticism makes thought ultimately *apply* to action exclusively—to con-

ceived action," but this does not make thought or the ultimate purpose of thought "to consist in acts." Rather, the "purport lies in "conditional general resolutions to act" (*CP* 5.402 n. 3). Here, however, he is using "schemata" not as involving generality but in the Kantian sense which he came to reject. Ultimately, for Peirce, schemata provide the means of becoming aware of the conditional resolutions to action embodied in living habit, and thus he came to recognize both that schemata are needed and that they cannot be particular. Here it is perhaps worth noting that it was in 1878 that Peirce rejected schemata because they lacked generality, while his pragmatic transformation of them developed in 1905.

45. *CP* 8.305.

46. Ibid.

47. *CP* 5.475.

48. *CP* 5.486.

49. *CP* 5.467.

50. Ibid.

51. *CP* 5.400, 5.491.

52. *CP* 4.9.

53. *CP* 8.326, 8.333.

54. See Altushuler, "Nature of Peirce's Pragmatism," 155.

55. This parallels the similar point made in the discussion of mathematics.

56. *CP* 6.132.

57. *CP* 5.491. Here "motive" seems analogous to "anticipated result."

58. Peter Krauser, "The Three Fundamental Structural Categories of Charles S. Peirce," *Transactions of the Charles S. Peirce Society: A Quarterly Journal in American Philosophy* 13 (1977): 209.

59. *CP* 6.152.

60. *CP* 7.498. By "general idea" here is of course meant not a Lockean type of generality but the generality of a schematic aspect.

61. *CP* 6.141.

62. Schematic image as appearance and as objective structure has implications for what Peirce calls the "percipuum" in its narrow sense and in its wide sense respectively. The dual aspects of the percipuum will be discussed later in this chapter.

63. See Karl-Otto Apel, *Charles S. Peirce: From Pragmatism to Pragmaticism*, trans. John Krois (Amherst: University of Massachusetts Press, 1981), 117.

64. Peirce, *New Elements of Mathematics*, 4.238.

65. *CP* 6.170. It should be noted that neither here within the logic of concepts nor within Peirce's metaphysical position is the individual the purely discrete; rather, the individual partakes of the nature of Thirdness

or generality. In the present instance, the "individual" appearances partake of the generality of human habit-taking. The metaphysical aspect of this point is developed in a later chapter.

66. *CP* 7.648. This will be discussed later in the chapter.

67. There are levels of possibilities of verification involved in the logic of meaning structure. While a physical object concept contains, at one level, the structure of action-related objective characters, it also contains the structure of action-related appearance apprehensions. The difference among apprehended object, apprehended objective character, and apprehended appearance is a difference in meaning levels operative within the internal structure of a concept.

68. See the earlier discussion of mathematical containment.

69. Conditional "upon all the different possible circumstances" (*CP* 5.438).

70. Thus, in Peirce's famous statement "Consider what effects, that might conceivably have practical bearings, we conceive the object of our conception to have. Then our conception of these effects is the whole of our conception of the object," conceivable effects are conceivable kinds of effects and cannot be reduced to actual instances (*CP* 5.2).

71. Therefore, concepts are meaningful, but are themselves neither true nor false, though they may be validly or invalidly explicated in analytic propositions. Propositions asserting the empirical applicability of a meaning, or asserting empirical relations among meaningful objects or facts, are empirically true or false.

72. This point will be developed further in later chapters.

73. This is analogous to the "skeletonized" aspect of mathematical schemata (*CP* 2.778).

74. MS 637, p. 28.

75. Thompson, "Peirce's Verificationist Realism." See note 3 of this chapter.

76. *CP* 6.496.

77. *CP* 3.93.

78. Such an individual "thing" is not, ontologically, what Peirce means by an absolute individual, which "cannot exist, properly speaking" (*CP* 3.93, footnote). An absolute individual would be a bare reaction event, an abstraction from the concreteness of existence as a continuous process, as a continuity of events. Thus, the individual thing of perceptual experience, in its concreteness, is not an "absolute individual." See MS 478, pp. 47–48.

79. This, of course, has reference to Peirce's category of existence.

80. Appearances, it should be remembered, are meanings that serve as a verification level within the structure of dispositional meaning.

81. *CP* 8.195. As Peirce states, certain experiments are "logically

necessitated" to turn out in a certain way. Logical necessity lies in deductive, not empirical, relations.

82. Synonymy has not eclipsed containment in contemporary discussions, but synonymy occupies most of the spotlight because ultimately, it is thought, what is required is a complete analysis of what is contained in a concept, and this will have to be a statement of synonymy.

83. *CP* 2.710, 2.710 footnote.

84. *CP* 5.288.

85. Ibid.

86. *CP* 5.289.

87. *Charles Sanders Peirce: Contributions to the Nation,* compiled and annotated by Kenneth Lane Ketner and James Edward Cook (Lubbock, Tex.: Texas Tech Press, 1975–79), 3.188.

88. *CP* 5.288.

89. See *CP* 1.452, 2.233.

90. Peirce, *New Elements of Mathematics,* 3.850.

91. Here it must be remembered that, as stressed earlier, this analytic nature involves a predictive rule generative of the action-image matrix of a schematic structure. Thus, the abstract concepts of mathematics cannot be divorced from their rootedness in activity.

92. *CP* 4.232–33.

93. *CP* 4.480.

94. *CP* 2.96.

95. *CP* 5.491.

96. Israel Scheffler, *Four Pragmatists: A Critical Introduction to Peirce, James, Mead and Dewey* (New York: Humanities Press, 1974). These parallel assumptions pervade most of the book, either explicitly or implicitly.

97. Almeder, "Peirce on Meaning," 21.

98. Even mathematics has a type of empirical reference built into its meanings in terms of sensory marks; thus even mathematics has a type of sense imagery. Further, though we can "know all about" a mathematical meaning because we have created it, yet there is always more for creative reasoning to generate from it, there is always more contained in it.

99. Fred Michael, "The Deduction of Categories in Peirce's 'New List,'" *Transactions of the Charles S. Peirce Society: A Quarterly Journal in American Philosophy* 16 (1980), 207.

100. *CP* 4.447.

101. Peirce's cryptic discussion of the evolution of Platonic forms (*CP* 6.194) is apt here. Evolving concepts are analogous to "Platonic Forms," not in the sense of being metaphysical essences, but in the sense that each successive concept can itself be characterized as fixed, eternal,

unchanging and, indeed, "toward the side of math." This point was made in the previous chapter, but the internal structure of meaning that accounts for this was not there developed.

102. *CP* 2.302.

103. *CP* 2.352.

104. *CP* 8.191, 2.29. This point was developed in the previous chapter in the context of the discussion of world. With that discussion in mind, it is important to note that this does not provide an "absolute truth" based on the "inconceivability of its negation"—a position emphatically rejected by Peirce. It is an inconceivability based on what can and cannot fit consistently with the "facts" of experience as they have been thus far interpreted through the meanings we have established. Inconceivability is thus always relative to a context, which is itself subject to possible change. Further, such "relative inconceivability" is not the psychological criterion to which Peirce objects but rather the epistemic correlate of a logical contradiction—if correctly grasped—a condition that we can never know with certainty to have attained. Precisely the "single example" of "false inconceivability" that Peirce chooses to give is that of a wrongly explicated necessary truth, an error committed because the schematic possibilities of a mathematical hypothesis were not fully taken into account (*CP* 2.30).

105. *CP* 2.743.

106. There is of course a difference between the abductive formation of a meaning and the abductive hypothesis that a meaning is applicable to experience, or, in other terms, that this experience is an instance of a kind. This point was developed earlier in this chapter.

107. Peirce points out that "containing-contained" is not a convertible relation (*CP* 2.718).

108. *CP* 1.140. Thus, chance is always operative in the universe.

109. *CP* 2.721.

110. For Peirce, perceptual judgments are extreme cases of abductive inferences or hypothesis formations (*CP* 5.181, 2.96).

111. The analytic proposition and the empirical generalization are usually indistinguishable by their form. Both are universal in intent, and they are normally expressed by an "all" proposition or by one in which the "all," though unexpressed, is implicit. The difference between them is the difference between the intensional and extensional "all." The first expresses a relation of logical containment; the second expresses an empirical connection between two classes of objects or two types of facts, the meanings of which are not related intensionally.

112. *CP* 4.71.

113. MS 290, pp. 2–3.

114. *CP* 5.475.

115. *CP* 8.119, 8.191.

116. T. L. Short, "What they said in Amsterdam: Peirce's Semiotic Today," *Semiotica* 60 (1986): 110. Though Short also holds that Peirce's theory of meaning relates more properly to his pragmatism than to his semiotic ("Life among the Legisigns," *Transactions of the Charles S. Peirce Society: A Quarterly Journal in American Philosophy* 18 [1982]: 308), the present work views Peirce's pragmatism, theory of meaning, and semiotic as being inextricably interrelated.

117. *Semiotics and Significs: The Correspondence between Charles S. Peirce and Victoria Lady Welby,* ed. Charles S. Hardwick (Bloomington: Indiana University Press, 1977), 80.

118. The role of imagination is discussed at some length by J. E. Tiles in "Iconic Thought and the Scientific Imagination," *Transactions of the Charles S. Peirce Society: A Quarterly Journal in American Philosophy* 24 (1988): 161.

119. Klaus Oehler, "Is a Transcendental Foundation of Semiotics Possible? A Peircean Consideration," *Transactions of the Charles S. Peirce Society: A Quarterly Journal in American Philosophy* 23 (1987): 59.

120. Almeder, *Philosophy of Charles S. Peirce,* 32.

121. *CP* 5.476, 5.491.

122. As indicated above, the logical interpretant is the mark of the habit or ultimate logical interpretant.

123. *CP* 4.536. See also *CP* 8.314.

124. *CP* 8.179ff.

125. *CP* 8.178.

126. Peirce and Welby, *Semiotics and Significs,* 72.

127. While these possibilities and constraints of resistance can at times be experienced at least partially independent of conceptual ordering into particular types of objectivities, this is of course not "pure acquaintance," for there is no experience for Peirce that is devoid of at least minimal interpretation. This point will be developed more fully below.

128. This point is similar in spirit to Carl Hausman's use of the terms *positive and negative vectors.* (Carl Hausman, "Metaphorical Reference and Peirce's Dynamical Object, *Transactions of the Charles S. Peirce Society: A Quarterly Journal of American Philosophy* 23 [1987]: 389ff.).

129. In *CP* 5.476 and 5.491 Peirce is obviously using "the ultimate logical interpretant" and "the final logical interpretant" interchangeably. At other times, however, he distinctly holds a difference to exist between them. See, for example, *CP* 8.184. Whether or not Peirce ultimately intends a difference is difficult to discern, especially in light of the insightful arguments pro and con given by two of the most astute interpreters of

Peirce's semiotic in their disagreement over this issue. (In *Transactions of the Charles S. Peirce Society: A Quarterly Journal in American Philosophy* 22 [1986], see T. L. Short, "David Savan's Peirce Studies," 104–8, and David Savan, "Response to T. L. Short," 138–42.) Such a distinction, however, seems justifiable, in true pragmatic fashion, in light of its workability within the structure of Peirce's overall position.

130. T. L. Short, "Semeiosis and Intentionality," *Transactions of the Charles Peirce Society: A Quarterly Journal in American Philosophy* 17 (1981): 219.

131. *CP* 2.96.

132. *CP* 1.171–72. This point was utilized in chapter 1 and will be developed in some detail in chapter 5.

133. *CP* 8.314.

134. *CP* 5.311. Emphasis added. The significance of this point was mentioned in the previous chapter and will be further developed in chapter 5.

135. There is no intent here to parallel the immediate object with the immediate interpretant. The use of the term *immediate* by Peirce for characterizations of both is unfortunate.

136. Peirce and Welby, *Semiotics and Significs,* 80–81.

137. Ibid., 111.

138. *CP* 8.315.

139. In comparing Lady Welby's "Sense" with his own Immediate Interpretant, which Peirce takes to be "very nearly, if not quite the same," he states that "Since you say it is Sensual and has no Volitional element, I suppose it is of the nature of an 'impression'. It is thus, as far as I can see, exactly my Immediate Interpretant" (Peirce and Welby, *Semiotics and Significs,* 110).

140. *CP* 5.289.

141. This feature of schematic structure, discussed earlier, will be developed more fully and from a different direction in the following analysis of the perceptual judgment.

142. As seen earlier, Peirce holds that there are no first impressions of sense.

143. James Jakob Liszak, in "Peirce's Interpretant," touches upon this interrelation in several illuminating ways. (*Transactions of the Charles S. Peirce Society: A Quarterly Journal in American Philosophy* 26 [1990]: 17–62.)

144. Although the above analysis has not dealt with dynamical objects as fictive objects, it may give some direction for understanding, in part, the coerciveness of fictive dynamical objects. The constraints imposed by fictive dynamical objects lie partially in the fact that what count as constraints are determined by the ultimate logical interpretant that lets

the object, "Hamlet's insanity" be as an object, while the ultimate logical interpretant must produce schematic aspects that work in the context of the "Universe of Shakespeare's Creation." Further, "Hamlet's insanity," as well as the "Universe of Shakespeare's Creation" must be understood in terms of collateral experience of Hamlet's attributes, as well as of the attributes of the Universe of Shakespeare's Creation, without which neither Hamlet nor the context can be understood. And this collateral experience, coming ultimately from real rather than fictive attributes, imparts its coercive and collateral nature to fictive dynamical objects. Even a characterization deliberately meant to contradict perceptual experience is constrained by, and can be understood to contradict only in terms of, past perceptual experience and the collateral experience of dynamical objects that it involves. (See *CP* 8.183, 8.178 for Peirce's discussion of these points.) Such a line of interpretation is quite different than Douglas Greenlee's assimilation of a fictive dynamical object to a previous internal thought, *Peirce's Concept of Sign* (The Hague: Mouton Press, 1973), 65–66, an assimmilation with which Carl Hausman rightly, I think, takes issue in "Metaphorical Reference and Peirce's Dynamical Object."

145. Hookway, *Peirce,* 166.

146. David Gruender, "Pragmatism, Science, and Metaphysics," in *The Relevance of Charles Peirce,* ed. Eugene Freeman (La Salle, Ill.: Hegeler Institute, 1983), 281–87.

147. Jeremiah McCarthy, "Peirce's Proof of Pragmatism," *Transactions of the Charles S. Peirce Society: A Quarterly Journal in American Philosophy* 26 (1990), 63–113.

148. Carl Hausman, "In and Out of Percepts," *Transactions of the Charles S. Peirce Society: A Quarterly Journal in American Philosophy* 26 (1990) 271–308.

149. It is also held, though the point will not be pressed, that this present way of extrapolating has more support in the actual texts than do other ways.

150. Carl Hausman's analysis of two meanings of the perceptual judgment in Peirce's philosophy does not correspond with the distinction being made here ("In and Out of Percepts," 271–308).

151. *CP* 7.642–81. Peirce's late introduction of this term has been noted by Richard Bernstein in "Peirce's Theory of Perception," in *Studies in the Philosophy of Charles Sanders Peirce,* 2d ser., ed. Edward Moore and Richard Robin (Amherst: University of Massachusetts Press, 1964), 175.

152. *CP* 7.642.

153. *CP* 7.676.

154. *CP* 7.675.

155. *CP* 7.648.

156. Hookway, *Peirce,* 166. Surprisingly, Hookway does not pursue this point.

157. Ibid.

158. Peirce at times makes a distinction between impressions and sensations. As he states, "No one can know what an impression is like in itself . . . an impression in itself is an undifferentiated sensation" (*Writings,* 1.515). In keeping with this distinction, the ponecipuum would serve as the vehicle for transforming impressions into recognizable, differentiated sensations. Since Peirce more often interchanges the terms *impression* and *sensation,* however, the introduction of this distinction would only lend confusion to some of the issues to be discussed in later chapters.

159. MS 740.

160. Ibid.

161. The ponecipuum would thus serve to transform a instantaneous, indescribable medad into recognizable monadic content. For a more detailed characterization of medads and their relation to monads see Carl Hausman's "In and Out of Percepts," 287–93.

162. *CP* 7.677.

163. *CP* 2.143.

164. This point will be further developed in the discussion of Firstness in chapter 5.

165. It cannot be overemphasized that the present analysis is abstracting discernable dimensions from what is a continuous process. Thus, "follows upon" as well as other such terminology should not be taken to indicate discrete elements.

166. *CP* 1.357. Firstness will be examined in some detail in chapter 5.

167. *CP* 7.629.

168. Ibid.

169. *CP* 7.628.

170. Ibid. Emphasis added.

171. (*CP* 7.636n) from alternative pages of the manuscript.

172. *CP* 5.54.

173. *CP* 7.634–35.

174. Roderick Chisholm, "Fallibilism and Belief," in *Studies in the Philosophy of Charles Sanders Peirce,* ed. Philip Wiener and Frederic Young (Cambridge: Harvard University Press, 1952), 105.

175. *CP* 5.544. Emphasis added.

176. *CP*5.545.

177. Ibid.

178. *CP* 5.544.

179. Bernstein "Peirce's Theory of Perception," 175.

180. Ibid., 173.

181. McCarthy, "Peirce's Proof of Pragmatism," 63–113. McCarthy's highly perceptive analysis goes astray here because he remains too general in his discussion of perceptual judgments.

182. Thus Peirce states that both conceptions and sensations involve hypothetical inferences

183. Peirce, *Writings* 1.471.

184. Gruender, in his foundationalist interpretation of Peirce's position ("Pragmatism, Science, and Metaphysics," 281–87), views the interrelation of observation and theory in Peirce's philosophy in terms of types of language, and he seems to place the infiltration of the theoretical into what is given at a more sophisticated level than is indicated here. Thus, he may well object both to the terminology and the concept that it indicates.

185. *CP* 5.265.

186. *CP* 5.442.

187. David Savan, "Decision and Knowledge in Peirce," *Transactions of the C. S. Peirce Society: A Quarterly Journal in American Philosophy* 1 (:1965): 40–41.

188. *CP* 5.158.

189. Peirce and Welby, *Semiotics and Significs,* 111. Emphasis in the original text.

3. HABIT, TEMPORALITY, AND PEIRCE'S PROOFS OF REALISM

1. Arthur Burks, "The Pragmatic-Humean Theory of Probability and Lewis's theory," in *The Philosophy of C. S. Lewis,* ed. Paul Schilpp, Library of Living Philosophers Series (La Salle Ill.: Open Court, 1968), 462. He levels this charge explicitly at both Lewis and Peirce.

2. Peter Turley, *Peirce's Cosmology* (New York: Philosophical Library, 1977), 56.

3. This claim was originally stated by Arthur Burks. It was defended by Edward Madden in "Chance and Counterfacts in Wright and Peirce," *Review of Metaphysics* 9 (1955–56).

4. Peter Skagestad, "Pragmatic Realism: The Peircean Argument Re-examined," *The Review of Metaphysics* 33 (1980): 527–40; see also, Skagestad, *The Road of Inquiry,* 134ff. It should be noted that the realism under discussion is that type of realism that lies in opposition to nominalism. It is not the realism that is contrasted with idealism.

5. Haack, "Extreme Scholastic Realism," 24.

6. Ibid., 24–28.

7. As was seen in chapter 2, "Meaning enters into language by determining it." MS 1105, p. 4.

8. This point was developed in part in chapter 2, but it will be taken up again in various ways throughout the remainder of this work.

9. The importance of temporality was hinted at in chapter 2, though it was not there developed.

10. It will be seen that Skagestad partially resolves one supposed contradiction, but he claims a remaining one is unavoidable.

11. *CP* 6.327.

12. The "uniformity of nature" is of course asserted by nominalists as well as realists.

13. John Boler serves as an example of a scholar who takes this approach (*Charles Peirce and Scholastic Realism* [Seattle: University of Washington Press, 1963], 111).

14. *CP* 4.45.

15. Peirce himself changed in his understanding of this issue in his earlier and later discussion of the diamond's hardness (*CP* 5.403, 5.457, 8.208). For an account of Peirce's own early nominalism see *Peirce, Semeiotic, and Pragmatism: Essays by Max H. Fisch,* ed. Kenneth Laine Ketner and Christian J. W. Kloesel (Bloomington: Indiana University Press, 1986), 368ff., and Fisch's introduction to the second volume of *Writings of Charles S. Peirce: A Chronological Edition,* xxv–xxviii.

16. Murphey, *Development of Peirce's Philosophy,* 395.

17. MS 137, p. 7.

18. *CP* 5.205.

19. Peirce identifies continuity with generality. See, for example, *CP* 6.173, 6.172. And, of course, these relate to the causal potentialities of Thirdness, not to the efficient causality of Secondness (*CP* 1.211).

20. Almeder, "Peirce on Meaning," 4.

21. *CP* 5.467.

22. *CP* 6.170, 6.138.

23. *CP* 6.138.

24. *CP* 6.141.

25. *CP* 6.139.

26. *CP* 5.3; quoted in Skagestad, "Pragmatic Realism," 532.

27. Ibid., 533.

28. Though a plan may be abductively formed in the light of past instances, it is always more than a collection of instances, for it is structured by habit as a rule of generation and organization of that which has been creatively or abductively "fixated"; thus at the core of the plan is the felt potentiality inherent in habit.

29. Thompson, "Peirce's Verificationist Realism," 87–93.

30. *CP* 5.457.
31. *CP* 7.675.
32. Ibid.
33. *CP* 7.649.
34. Robert Roth, "Did Peirce Answer Hume on Necessary Connection?" *The Review of Metaphysics* 38 (1985): 877–79.
35. MS 137, p. 10.
36. *CP* 5.96.
37. Manley Thompson, "Peirce's Experimental Proof of Scholastic Realism," *Studies in the Philosophy of Charles Sanders Peirce,* 2d ser., ed. Edward Moore and Richard Robin (Amherst: University of Massachusetts Press, 1964), 414ff.
38. Skagestad, "Pragmatic Realism," 535–36.
39. Ibid., 536.
40. *CP* 6.399.
41. *CP* 6.404–6.
42. Ibid.
43. This interpretation of Peirce gains support from his criticism of Mill concerning the uniformity of nature. Supra, chapter 1.
44. Though a chance world is logically possible in itself, when combined with information concerning the nature of mind as interpretive activity and the nature of uniformity as related to this activity, a logically impossible set results. This is not an a priori inconceivability, but an inconceivability based on what can and cannot fit consistently with the "facts" of experience as they have been thus far interpreted. This point was developed in chapter 1.
45. *CP* 6.407.
46. *CP* 6.406.
47. Ibid.
48. MS 350, Lect. 1.
49. MS 137, p. 13.
50. *CP* 4.641.
51. Skagestad, "Pragmatic Realism," 536.
52. MS 644, pp. 11–12.
53. Skagestad, "Pragmatic Realism," 537.
54. Ibid.
55. *CP* 7.671. What is given at an instant is not, for Peirce, a perspective of an object, for that requires the durational time within which habit functions.
56. *CP* 5.181, 2.96. Here it should be stressed that this shading of scientific abductions into everyday perceptual claims is a continuity not of content organized but of method of organization.
57. *CP* 5.212.

58. This latter point will be further developed in the following chapters.

59. Peirce's claim of the inconceivability of a chance world of course is not meant to deny the element of chance in the universe that negates necessitarianism.

60. The terms *ontological* and *metaphysical* are used interchangeably in this work. Although Peirce at times makes a distinction, seeming to label as "metaphysical" issues that are pragmatically "meaningless gibberish" or at best unsolvable, he is far from consistent in this use.

61. *CP* 5.464. Emphasis added.

62. *CP* 5.496.

63. MS 319, p. 5.

64. Alborn, "Peirce's Evolutionary Logic," 5.

65. 5.496.

4. PRAGMATIC EXPERIMENTALISM AND THE DERIVATION OF THE CATEGORIES

1. Murphey, *Development of Peirce's Philosophy.*

2. Thomas Goudge, *The Thought of C. S. Peirce* (Toronto: University of Toronto Press, 1950).

3. *CP* 1.535.

4. *CP* 1.288.

5. *CP* 1.353.

6. *CP* 1.287.

7. *CP* 1.284.

8. *CP* 5.122.

9. Peirce similarly uses the term *existence* in a broad sense as well as in the more narrow sense, which limits it to "one of the three Universes" (MS 137, pp. 2–4).

10. *CP* 7.535, 7.527.

11. *CP* 7.527.

12. *CP* 7.538. Peirce emphasizes that this "matter of sense" is "a hypothetical something which we never can seize as such, free from all interpetative working over" (Ibid.).

13. *CP* 1.321. In *CP* 5.37 Peirce states that he will not restrict phenomenology to the observation of experience, but he is there hitting what he considers to be Hegel's muddling of Secondness and Thirdness, "fact and essence," and thus uses experience in a more limited, technical sense.

14. *CP* 8.297.

15. *CP* 5.42.

16. *CP* 1.383.
17. *CP* 6.9.
18. *CP* 6.7.
19. *CP* 6.8.
20. Ibid.
21. *CP* 6.9.
22. Ibid.
23. *CP* 8.295. By "psychology" here Peirce means explanations "by motions and changes of the brain . . . a sort of physiology of the mind." (8.303)
24. *CP* 6.32.
25. *CP* 6.34.
26. *CP* 1.299.
27. Phenomenology is also dependent upon mathematics in that it requires "the generalizing power of the mathematician who produces the abstract formula that comprehends the very essence of the feature under examination purified from all admixture of extraneous and irrelevant accompaniments" (*CP* 5.42).
28. *CP* 5.40. He again objects to Hegel in a way not unrelated to the objection indicated in note 13: "A phenomenology which does not reckon with pure mathematics, a science hardly come to years of discretion when Hegel wrote, will be the same pitiful club-footed affair that Hegel produced." (Ibid)
29. *CP* 1.299.
30. *CP* 1.301.
31. *CP* 1.374. Since he is here referring to the triad in psychology, the facts will be psychological facts.
32. Peirce, *Writings*, 1.72–73.
33. *CP* 6.590.
34. *CP* 1.374.
35. *CP* 5.504.
36. *CP* 5.480.
37. *CP* 6.34.
38. As Peirce stated already in 1861: "If conceptions which are incapable of definition are simple, I, It, and Thou are so. Who could define either of these words, easy as they are to understand? Who does not perceive, in fact, that neither of them can be expressed in terms of the others? . . . Though they cannot be expressed in terms of each other, yet they have a relation to each other, for THOU is an IT in which there is another I. I looks in. It looks out, Thou looks *through*, out and in again. I outwells, It inflows, Thou commingles. . . . The I, the IT and the THOU are . . . in Three different worlds" (*Writings*, 1.45–46).
39. Murphey, *Development of Peirce's Philosophy*, 88.

40. Ibid., 89, 319. This general point is made concerning both the move to the New List and to the revised list.

41. *CP* 4.3.

42. Ibid.

43. Goudge, *Thought of C. S. Peirce,* 80, 268ff.

44. David Savan, "On the Origins of Peirce's Phenomenology," *Studies in the Philosophy of Charles Sanders Peirce,* ed. Philip Wiener and Frederic Young (Cambridge: Harvard University Press, 1952), 194.

45. Peirce applies his categories to various areas: "In psychology Feeling is First, Sense of reaction Second, General conception Third, or mediation. In biology, the idea of arbitrary sporting is First, heredity is Second, the process whereby the accidental characters become fixed is Third" (*CP* 6.32).

46. See Murphey, *Development of Peirce's Philosophy,* 368.

47. John Dewey, "Peirce's Theory of Quality," *Journal of Philosophy* 32 (1935), 702.

48. Goudge, *Thought of C. S. Peirce,* 77.

49. Andre De Tienne, in "Peirce's Early Method of Finding the Categories," concludes, after a detailed examination, that the method can best be characterized as "critical commonsensist retroduction" (*Transactions of the Charles S. Peirce Society: A Quarterly Journal in American Philosophy* 25 [1989]: 385–406). Although his analysis takes him in a direction different than that offered here, he sees that "some of the germs of Peirce's pragmaticism were already at work in his 'New List of Categories'" (Ibid., 405).

50. *CP* 1.525–26.

51. Peirce holds that the "several very broad classes of phanerons" are so inextricably mixed together that no one can be isolated, yet it is manifest that their characters are quite disparate" (*CP* 1.286). The traits, or classes of phenomena, are thus separable by precision, by attending to one element and neglecting others (see *CP* 1.353). Further, though Peirce speaks of "elements," what is intended is not analysis into elements but the tracing out of relations (*CP* 1.294).

52. MS 296, p. 16.

53. *CP* 1.525.

54. *CP* 1.526.

55. *CP* 5.82.

56. *CP* 5.119.

57. *CP* 5.121.

58. There is implied here a rejection of ontological phenomenalism. The issue of ontological phenomenalism concerns the objective reference of the contents of awareness. As indicated earlier in chapter 2, ontological phenomenalism holds that the contents of awareness—at

whatever level of complexity they are grasped—are either the only reality there is or the only reality that can be known, rather than a grasp of a "hard," external, independent reality.

59. MS 14, Article 23, p. 33.

60. *CP* 7.629.

61. *CP* 5.166.

62. *CP* 5.312.

63. *CP* 1.420.

64. *CP* 5.283.

65. *CP* 1.300.

66. *CP* 1.487.

67. *CP* 5.423.

68. *CP* 5.294.

69. Ibid.

70. *CP* 1.548.

71. *CP* 1.23.

72. *CP* 6.34.

73. *CP* 5.121.

74. Ibid., *CP* 5.124.

75. *CP* 6.342.

76. A second and related issue, which may well account for another of Peirce's dual characterizations of reality, was discussed in chapter 1.

77. There is intended here no ontological or numerical distinction between these two dimensions of reality. This point was clarified in some detail in chapter 1.

78. *CP* 5.565.

79. *CP* 5.316.

80. *CP* 5.405.

81. *CP* 5.407. The nature of this "ultimate opinion" was examined in chapter 1.

82. *CP* 1.282.

83. Justus Buchler, *Charles Peirce's Empiricism* (New York: Octagon Books, 1966), 151.

84. See chapter 1.

85. *CP* 6.2.

86. When Peirce speaks of premisses and conclusions, he is indicating the direction of abduction, not deduction, or in other terms, the order of discovery, not the order of logical analysis. Thus, the premisses are the observed data, while the conclusions are the abductive hypotheses from the data.

87. Ibid.

88. See Nynfa Bosco, "Peirce and Metaphysics," in *Studies in the*

Philosophy of Charles Sanders Peirce, 2d ser., ed. Edward Moore and Richard Robin (Amherst: University of Massachusetts Press, 1964), 352.

89. MS 284, pp. 68–69.

90. *CP* 1.316.

91. *CP* 5.356. Emphasis in the original text.

92. Philip Wiener, "Peirce's Evolutionary Interpretations of the History of Science," *Studies in the Philosophy of Charles Sanders Peirce,* ed. Philip Wiener and Frederic Young (Cambridge: Harvard University Press, 1952), 145.

93. Richard Bernstein notes Peirce's own "extremely fertile imagination" at work in the very grouping of the various and diverse phenomena which are brought together under each of the three categories. "Action, Conduct, and Self-Control," in *Perspectives on Peirce,* ed. Richard J. Bernstein (New Haven: Yale University Press, 1965), 73.

94. MS 283, p. 132.

95. MS 870, p. 6.

96. MS 283, p. 132.

97. See chapter 2.

98. MS 403, p. 22.

99. *CP* 5.196.

100. *CP* 5.356.

101. MS 290, pp. 30–31.

102. *CP* 1.217.

103. *CP* 1.129.

104. *CP* 1.7.

105. *CP* 1.6.

106. Victor Lowe, "Pierce and Whitehead as Metaphysicians," in *Studies in the Philosophy of Charles Sanders Peirce,* 2d ser., ed. Edward Moore and Richard Robin (Amherst: University of Massachusetts Press, 1964), 444.

107. A. N. Whitehead, *Process and Reality* (New York: Harper and Brothers, 1957), 4.

108. Helmut Pape notes that "Peirce's claim that all human thought has an anthropomorphic character" has methodological implications and implies an idealistic metaphysics ("Laws of Nature," 211). While the anthropomorphic character of thought has implications for the *method* of metaphysical endeavor, however, it need not, as Pape holds, require the *content* of metaphysics to be that of objective idealism.

109. Smith, *Purpose and Thought,* 126.

110. Murray Murphey, "On Pierce's Metaphysics," *Transactions of the Charles Sanders Peirce Society: A Quarterly Journal in American Philosophy* 1 1965), 13.

111. *CP* 1.10.

5. PEIRCE'S PRAGMATIC METAPHYSICS: THE FOUNDATION FOR PLURALISM

1. Smith, *Purpose and Thought,* 126.

2. Pape, "Laws of Nature," 209. Pape finds Peirce's evolutionary cosmology to involve objective idealism, which is not the direction taken by the present interpretation.

3. See chapter 3.

4. MS 288, p. 189.

5. *CP* 5.44, 1.547.

6. *CP* 8.301. Emphasis added. Whether or not Peirce's understanding of James's position here is accurate is irrelevant for the present purpose.

7. *CP* 7.649.

8. *CP* 6.126. The present in general is not the abstraction of the bare reaction event of secondness; it includes Firstness and Thirdness as well, for it is a durational flow that incorporates both past and future. This point will be discussed more directly later in the chapter.

9. William L. Rosensohn holds that there is a contradiction in Peirce's thought precisely because he views Peirce's metaphysical categories as "separated modes of reality" rather than as having the "interdependent and universally present" character of the phenomenological categories (*The Phenomenology of Charles S. Peirce* [Amsterdam: B. R. Gruner, 1974], 87).

10. Isabel Stearn, "Firstness, Secondness, and Thirdness," in *Studies in the Philosophy of Charles Sanders Pierce,* ed. Philip Wiener and Frederic Young (Cambridge: Harvard University Press, 1952), 196–97.

11. Hookway, *Peirce,* 106.

12. Boler, *Charles Peirce and Scholastic Realism,* 122–23.

13. That Firstness is elusive is surely true. It has often been said, however, that its characterization is inherently inconsistent. This statement is debatable, and it is largely rejected by the present interpretation. The charge of inconsistency is based both on Peirce's diverse characterizations of Firstness (see, e.g., Thomas A. Goudge, "The Views of Charles Peirce on the Given in Experience," *Journal of Philosophy,* 32 [1935]: 538) and on his change in emphasis between earlier and later writings (see, e.g., Murphey, *Development of Peirce's Philosophy,* 306–7.)

14. *CP* 6.222.

15. *CP* 6.231.

16. *CP* 7.624.

17. Murphey, *Development of Peirce's Philosophy,* 307.

18. *CP* 6.224.

19. 1.302 The awareness of qualities as repeatable and recognizable

qualia is still a more primitive epistemological level than that of the awareness of qualities as objective properties indicating possibilities of future experience. The only type of possibilities of future experience inherent in repeatable qualia is the possibility of repetition. Here, however, it should be noted that qualities as qualia and qualities as objective properties are meant to be not numerically distinct but epistemologically distinct. They represent different levels of interpretation.

20. *CP* 6.236.
21. *CP* 1.357.
22. *CP* 5.444.
23. *CP* 1.310.
24. Murphey, *Development of Peirce's Philosophy,* 339.
25. MS 739, p. 30.
26. *CP* 1.357.
27. See previous chapter for Peirce's reliance on this method.
28. *CP* 1.311.
29. This view lies implicit in the previous analysis of the perceptual judgment in its analytically narrow sense.
30. *CP* 7.392. This reference to ideas of sensations is perhaps a good example of Peirce's often confused way of speaking. However, the general direction of his thought seems clear enough.
31. Qualia, as "alike to the comparing consciousness," are in one sense the most abstract elements of the phenomenon, though this does not contradict their characterization as Firsts. The recognized qualia are the most abstract of the phenomena in the sense in which abstraction is equated with precision. By abstraction or precision Peirce means a mental separation that "arises from attention to one element and neglect of the other." (*CP* 1.549) The term *precision* as used by Peirce is the cognate of the verb *prescind,* not the adjective *precise.* As Peirce states elsewhere, what he intends can best be expressed by the term *precission.* (*CP* 2.42) Furthermore, in this latter passage Peirce stresses that the process of precision is not that by which we obtain, for example, the abstract concept, whiteness, but rather that by which we are able to grasp a white appearance generally, or, in other terms, to recognize a quale as an instance of a kind. And, in this sense, qualia, as the recognizable but ineffable elements in experience are the most abstract of the phenomena of experience and of the nature of Firstness, for while pure abstraction can be reached by the agreement of things in some respect, Peirce denies the relativity of Firstness to anything else by which it is grasped. Thus, in its phenomenological sense, a First is an immediately recognized quale.
32. *CP* 6.236.
33. *CP* 6.227. That Peirce characterizes the quale-element, which appears "upon the inside as unity, and upon the outside as variety," as the

same logical element is merely a recognition of the fact that this distinction is not needed if one is considering only the logical or epistemological function of qualia in cognition. This point relates to the previous analysis of perceptual experience.

34. L. Edward Allemand, "Peirce's Notion of Firstness and French Phenomenology," in *Proceedings of the Charles S. Peirce Bicentennial International Congress,* ed. Kenneth Ketner, Joseph Ransdell, Carolyn Eisele, Max Fisch, and Charles Hardwick (Lubbock, Tex.: Texas Tech Press, 1981), 76.

35. *CP* 5.213, 7.465. See also chapter 2.

36. Peirce, *Writings,* 1.515. See also MS 942, p. 8 for Peirce's understanding of a first impression of sense as a limit concept.

37. The terms *qualia* and *stimuli* are meant to indicate not a numerical distinction but a logical or epistemological distinction: qualitative richness as grasped by consciousness and as independent of consciousness respectively. Peirce holds quite emphatically to a theory of direct perception. See *CP* 5.56.

38. *CP* 1.422.

39. From the limited discussion thus far it can already be seen that firstness is at once, but without inconsistency, quality of feeling, ineffable and unknowable, and pure possibility. Furthermore, it is both quality determining a class and quality as the sensory element of experience. Diverse combinations of these various features have been held to point to inconsistencies in Peirce's characterization of Firstness. See note 13.

40. *CP* 1.536.

41. *CP* 4.547.

42. *CP* 1.42.

43. *CP* 1.304.

44. *CP* 2.664.

45. MS 277, p. 1.

46. *CP* 6.236.

47. *CP* 6.227.

48. Boler, *Charles Peirce and Scholastic Realism,* 158.

49. Ibid. 158 n. 18.

50. For a more detailed analysis of this claim, see chapter 1, note 24. See also Justus Buchler on this point (*Charles Peirce's Empiricism,* 25). (Peirce further holds that neither of these logical principles applies to possibilities.)

51. *CP* 5.505.

52. *CP* 2.83.

53. *CP* 8, p. 279.

54. N. A. Brian Noble, "Peirce's Definitions of Continuity and the

Concept of Possibility," *Transactions of the Charles S. Peirce Society: A Quarterly Journal in American Philosophy* 25 (1989): 170.

55. In *A History of Philosophy in America*, vol. 2 (New York: G. P. Putnam's Sons, 1977), Elizabeth Flower and Murray G. Murphey point out that Peirce describes feeling as being at least triply continuous: first, feelings endure and so are continuous in time; second, feelings admit of continuous variation with respect to their intensity; and third, feelings are spatially continuous (609). Feeling, however, is understood by them, as in Murphey's *Development of Peirce's Philosophy*, in the psychological rather than the epistemic sense.

56. *CP* 6.205.

57. *CP* 6.132.

58. Ibid.

59. *CP* 6.111.

60. See chapter 4.

61. *CP* 5.119.

62. See chapter 1 for a brief statement of this line of interpretation in relation to the issue of world.

63. W. P. Haas, *The Conception of Law and the Unity of Peirce's Philosophy* (Notre Dame: University of Notre Dame Press, 1964), 99; Quote incorporated from Peirce, *CP* 3.527.

64. Ibid.; *CP* 8.303 in Peirce.

65. Turley, *Peirce's Cosmology*, 88.

66. Bertrand Helm, *Time and Reality in American Philosophy* (Amherst: University of Massachusetts Press, 1985), 27–28.

67. *CP* 8.308.

68. It was seen in chapter 1 that neither does the ideal world, of which the sensible world is but a fragment, lend itself to a Platonic interpretation, except in a sort of Pickwickian sense. The ideal world is the conceptual world of the logically possible or the consistently thinkable within which the facts of experience must be located. To turn such a "conceptual world" into an "ontological world" is an unwarranted reification that leads to a static conception of the metaphysical possibilities of Firstness.

69. D. J. Bronstein, "Inquiry and Meaning," in *Studies in the Philosophy of C. S. Peirce*, ed. Philip Wiener and Frederic Young (Cambridge: Harvard University Press, 19542), 47.

70. Boler, *Charles Peirce and Scholastic Realism*, 153.

71. Wennerberg, *Pragmatism of C. S. Peirce*, 44.

72. *CP* 7.336.

73. *CP* 1.211.

74. *CP* 1.212.

75. Ibid.
76. *CP* 6.24.
77. *CP* 7.570.
78. *CP* 1.402.
79. *CP* 6.64.
80. *CP* 6.12.
81. *CP* 6.553–54.
82. *CP* 6.221.
83. *CP* 1.311.
84. This point was developed in chapter 4.
85. W. B. Gallie, *Peirce and Pragmatism* (New York: Dover Publications, 1966), 216.
86. *CP* 5.440.
87. Larry Holmes, "Peirce's Philosophy of Mind," in *Studies in the Philosophy of C. S. Peirce,* 2d ser., ed. Edward Moore and Richard Robin (Amherst: University of Massachusetts Press, 1985), 364.
88. *CP* 6.25.
89. *CP* 6.127.
90. *CP* 6.128.
91. *CP* 5.436.
92. *CP* 5.494.
93. Boler, *Charles Peirce and Scholastic Realism,* 3.
94. *CP* 1.16. Here it should be noted that the realism under discussion is that type of realism that is contrasted with nominalism. It is not the realism that lies in opposition to idealism. As seen in the above examination of Peirce's supposed idealism, it does not deny the facticity or brute "thereness" of an ongoing, open-ended universe. It denies only the dualistic or mechanistic interpretation of the universe that is "there." In "Two Forms of Scholastic Realism in Peirce's Philosophy," *Transactions of the Charles S. Peirce Society: A Quarterly Journal in American Philosophy* 24 (1988): 317–48, Fred Michael argues that Peirce's early and late realism differ with respect to the reality of universals outside the mind. Michael holds that the early realism was an attack against incognizable realities, things-in-themselves to which Peirce considered nominalists to be committed, while the later realism was positively committed to the reality of universals. Bruce Kuklick, on the other hand, argues that for Peirce it is metaphysical realism (presumably realism in Michael's first sense) that entails nominalism and materialism, and that Peirce was thus led to an epistemological realism that was "logically equivalent to a communitarian idealism" (*The Rise of American Philosophy* [New Haven: Yale University Press, 1977], 107). The second sense of realism indicated by Michael is the one presently under discussion, and it is of course an explicit rejection of nominalism. In this connection two points should

be noted. According to the present work, the very meaningfulness of this latter realism within the context of Peirce's pragmatism is intertwined with the rejection of things-in-themselves, nominalism, and materialism. And, the "universals" to which Peirce is committed cannot be understood in any traditional sense. Epistemically, they are functions of noetic activity, while metaphysically they are tendencies or dispositions of a processive reality.

95. *CP* 1.19.

96. *CP* 8.208. Duns Scotus, as well as other traditional scholastic realists, will all seem to fall under the broad rubric of what Susan Haack so aptly calls "nominalistic Platonism." "Extreme Scholastic Realism," 33.

97. *CP* 1.213.

98. *CP* 5.436.

99. *CP* 1.212.

100. Boler, *Charles Peirce and Scholastic Realism,* 115.

101. Ibid., 141; Boler is quoting *CP* 8.208.

102. Ibid., 142–43.

103. Goudge, *Thought of C. S. Peirce,* 144.

104. Gallie, *Peirce and Pragmatism,* 225.

105. *CP* 1.427.

106. *CP* 1.531.

107. The "may-be" of Firstness as negative continuity or negative generality is also the "may-be" of Firstness as the qualitative aspect of reality. See *CP* 1.536.

108. *CP* 6.205.

109. *CP* 6.203.

110. Charles Hartshorne, "Charles Peirce's 'One Contribution to Philosophy' and His Most Serious Mistake," in *Studies in the Philosophy of Charles Sanders Peirce,* 2d ser., ed. Edward Moore and Richard Robin (Amherst: University of Massachusetts Press, 1964), 467.

111. *CP* 3.93n. Neither can the absolute individual, for Peirce, "be realized in sense or thought" (*CP* 3.93). This is not only because of the presently indicated nature of Secondness, but also because of both the universalizing aspect of sense and the indeterminateness of meaning, as discussed in previous chapters.

112. MS 462, p. 58.

113. *CP* 1.220.

114. For Peirce, "A true continuum is something whose possibilities of determination no multitude of individuals can exhaust" (*CP* 6.170).

115. *CP* 4.36, 5.107. Emphasis added.

116. *CP* 6.169ff.

117. This position seems supported by Carl Hausman's excellent and detailed discussion of continuity and infinitesimals, though he pushes the points in a somewhat different way. (*Charles Pierce's Evolutionary Philosophy,* 183–90).

118. *CP* 8.284.

119. Peirce's dual senses of reality were discussed in chapter 4.

120. Douglas Greenlee, "Peirce's Hypostatic and Factorial Categories," *Transactions of the Charles S. Peirce Society: A Quarterly Journal in American Philosophy* 4 (1968): 55, 58. It should here again be stressed that the present interpretation does not characterize the qualitative aspect of metaphysical Firstness as abstract, as does Greenlee; rather, this interpretation characterizes it as an infinitely rich concreteness. As seen earlier, Peirce's characterization of Firstness as abstract refers to an epistemological function, not an ontological status.

121. As indicated earlier in this chapter, "feeling" for Peirce indicates an epistemic level, not a psychological category.

122. *CP* 6.265.

123. *CP* 7.381.

124. *CP* 6.101.

125. *CP* 7.570.

126. *CP* 6.101.

127. Carl Hausman, "Eros and Agape in Creative Evolution: A Peircean Insight," *Process Studies* 4, no. 1 (1974): 11–25.

128. Douglas Anderson, in *Creativity and the Philosophy of C. S. Peirce* (Dordrecht: Martinus Nijhoff, 1987), also focuses on the radically creative nature of agape.

129. *CP* 6.63.

130. Ibid.

131. Hausman, "Eros and Agape in Creative Evolution," 15.

132. William James, *A Pluralistic Universe, The Works of William James,* ed. Frederick Burkhardt (Cambridge: Harvard University Press, 1975–), 153.

133. MS 942, p. 16.

134. Hausman, "Eros and Agape in Creative Evolution," 16–17.

135. The present position, as well as the alternative focus on agape, incorporates the importance of the fact that Peirce's own writings express the view that there are limitations on both mechanistic and teleological causal explanations of creative events (Hausman, "Eros and Agape in Creative Evolution," 14.) Vincent Potter argues in a way similar to Hausman's, claiming that "agapasm was necessary to avoid the extremes of tychistic evolution and its denial of continuity on the one hand, and anancastic evolution and its denial of spontaneity on the other (*Charles S.*

Peirce on Norms and Ideals [Amherst: University of Massachusetts Press, 1967], 171–90).

136. Bertrand Helm holds that Peirce's "account of time and time's domain lacks categories which could make sense of those aspects of human creativity that are revealed in poetry, literature, and drama." (*Time and Reality in American Philosophy,* 38). According to the present interpretation, Peirce's understanding of temporality is precisely what makes possible the radical creativity which is part and parcel of Peirce's pragmatic understanding of both human activity and the universe within which it functions.

137. For an excellent discussion of this view of human freedom in Peirce's philosophy, see Vincent M. Colapietro, *Peirce's Approach to the Self: A Semiotic Perspective on Human Subjectivity* (Albany: State University of New York Press, 1989), 99–118.

138. In chapter 3 the *sense* of freedom within human experience was discussed, but not the metaphysical conditions that allow for the reality of human freedom.

139. This point relates directly to the claim, in chapter 1, that while Peirce is neither an idealist nor a phenomenalist, the term *realism* as descriptive of his position is misleading because of the qualifications that must be made.

140. *CP* 1.171–72. This characterization by Peirce was mentioned in the discussions of world in chapter 1 and the dynamical object in chapter 2.

BIBLIOGRAPHY OF WORKS CITED

PRIMARY SOURCE

Charles Sanders Peirce: Contributions to the Nation. 3 vols. Compiled and annotated by Kenneth Lane Ketner and James Edward Cook. Lubbock, Tex.: Texas Tech Press, 1975–79.

Collected Papers of Charles Sanders Peirce. Vols. 1–6. Ed. Charles Hartshorne and Paul Weiss. Cambridge: Belknap Press of Harvard University, 1931–35.

Collected Papers of Charles Sanders Peirce. Vols. 7 and 8. Ed. Arthur Burks. Cambridge: Harvard University Press, 1958. (Cited in the text as *CP*.)

The Microfilm Edition of the Peirce Papers. Houghton Library, Harvard University. (Cited in the text by manuscript and page numbers.)

The New Elements of Mathematics. 4 vols, Ed. Carolyn Eisele. The Hague: Mouton Press, 1976.

Semiotics and Significs: The Correspondence between Charles S. Peirce and Victoria Lady Welby. Ed. Charles S. Hardwick. Bloomington: Indiana University Press, 1977.

Writings of Charles S. Peirce: A Chronological Edition. Bloomington: Indiana University Press, 1982–.

SECONDARY SOURCES

Alborn, Timothy. "Peirce's Evolutionary Logic: Continuity, Indeterminacy, and the Natural Order." *Transactions of the Charles S. Peirce Society: A Quarterly Journal in American Philosophy* 25 (1989).

Allemand, L. Edward. "Peirce's Notion of Firstness and French Phenomenology," in *Proceedings of the Charles S. Peirce Bicentennial International Congress,* ed. Kenneth Ketner, Joseph Ransdell, Carolyn Eisele, Max Fisch, and Charles Hardwick. Lubbock, Tex.: Texas Tech Press, 1981.

Almeder, Robert. "The Epistemological Realism of Charles Peirce." *Transactions of the Charles Peirce Society: A Quarterly Journal in American Philosophy* 11 (1975).

———. "Fallibilism and the Ultimate Irreversible Opinion." *American Philosophical Quarterly Monograph* no. 9 (1975).

———. "Peirce on Meaning." *Synthese* 41 (1979).

———. "Peirce's Thirteen Theories of Truth." *Transactions of the Charles S. Peirce Society: A Quarterly Journal in American Philosophy* 21 (1985).

———. *The Philosophy of Charles S. Peirce.* New Jersey: Rowman and Littlefield, 1980.

———. "Scientific Progress and Peircean Utopian Realism." *Erkenntnis* 20 (1983).

Altuschuler, Bruce. "The Nature of Peirce's Pragmatism." *Transactions of the Charles S. Peirce Society: A Quarterly Journal in American Philosophy* 14 (1978).

———. "Peirce's Theory of Truth and the Revolt against Realism." *Transactions of the Charles S. Peirce Society: A Quarterly Journal in American Philosophy* 18 (1982).

Anderson, Douglas. *Creativity and the Philosophy of C. S. Peirce,* Dordrecht: Martinus Nijhoff, 1987.

Apel, Karl-Otto. *Charles S. Peirce: From Pragmatism to Pragmaticism.* Trans. John Krois. Amherst: University of Massachusetts Press, 1981.

Bernstein, Richard. "Action, Conduct, and Self-Control," in *Perspectives on Peirce,* ed. Richard J. Bernstein. New Haven: Yale University Press, 1965.

———. "Peirce's Theory of Perception," in *Studies in the Philosophy of Charles Sanders Peirce,* 2d ser., ed. Edward Moore and Richard Robin. Amherst: University of Massachusetts Press, 1964.

Boler, John. *Charles Peirce and Scholastic Realism.* Seattle: University of Washington Press, 1963.

Bosco, Nynfa. "Peirce and Metaphysics," in *Studies in the Philosophy of Charles Sanders Peirce,* 2d ser., ed. Edward Moore and Richard Robin. Amherst: University of Massachusetts Press, 1964.

Bronstein, D. J. "Inquiry and Meaning," in *Studies in the Philosophy of Charles Sanders Peirce,* ed. Philip Wiener and Frederic Young. Cambridge: Harvard University Press, 1952.

Buchler, Justus. *Charles Peirce's Empiricism.* New York: Octagon Books, 1966.

Burks, Arthur. "The Pragmatic-Humean Theory of Probability and Lewis's Theory," in *The Philosophy of C. S. Lewis,* ed Paul Schilpp. Library of Living Philosophers Series. La Salle, Ill.: Open Court, 1968.

Chisholm, Roderick. "Fallibilism and Belief," in *Studies in the Philoso-*

phy of Charles Sanders Peirce, ed. Philip Wiener and Frederic Young. Cambridge: Harvard University Press, 1952.

Colapietro, Vincent M. *Peirce's Approach to the Self: A Semiotic Perspective on Human Subjectivity.* Albany: State University of New York Press, 1989.

Delaney, C. F. *Science, Knowledge and Mind: A Study in the Philosophy of C. S. Peirce.* Notre Dame and London: University of Notre Dame Press, 1993.

De Tienne, Andre. "Peirce's Early Method of Finding the Categories." *Transactions of the Charles S. Peirce Society: A Quarterly Journal in American Philosophy* 25 (1989).

Dewey, John. "Peirce's Theory of Quality." *Journal of Philosophy* 32 (1935).

Dozoretz, Jerry. "The Internally Real, the Fictitious, and the Indubitable," in *Studies in Peirce's Semiotic,* ed. Kenneth Ketner and Joseph Ransdell. Lubbock, Tex.: Institute for Studies in Pragmatism, 1979.

Esposito, Joseph. *Evolutionary Metaphysics: The Development of Peirce's Theory of Categories.* Athens: Ohio University Press, 1980.

Fisch, Max. *Peirce, Semeiotic, and Pragmatism: Essays by Max H. Fisch.* Ed. Kenneth Laine Ketner and Christian J. W. Kloesel. Bloomington: Indiana University Press, 1986.

Flower, Elizabeth, and Murray G. Murphey. *A History of Philosophy in America.* Vol. 2. New York: G. P. Putnam's Sons, 1977.

Gallie, W. B. *Peirce and Pragmatism.* New York: Dover Publications, 1966.

Goudge, Thomas. *The Thought of C. S. Peirce.* Toronto: University of Toronto Press, 1950.

______. "The Views of Charles Peirce on the Given in Experience." *Journal of Philosophy* 32 (1935).

Greenlee, Douglas. *Peirce's Concept of Sign.* The Hague: Mouton Press, 1973.

______. "Peirce's Hypostatic and Factorial Categories." *Transactions of the Charles S. Peirce Society: A Quarterly Journal in American Philosophy* 4 (1968).

Gruender, David. "Pragmatism, Science and Metaphysics," in *The Relevance of Charles Peirce,* ed. Eugene Freeman. La Salle, Ill.: Hegeler Institute, 1983.

Haack, Susan. "Extreme Scholastic Realism: Its Relevance to Philosophy of Science Today." *Transactions of the Charles S. Peirce Society: A Quarterly Journal in American Philosophy* 28 (1992).

______. "Fallibilism and Necessity." *Synthese* 41 (1979).

Haas, W. P. *The Conception of Law and the Unity of Peirce's Philosophy.* Notre Dame: University of Notre Dame Press, 1964.

Hare, Peter, Organizer, "Perspectives on the History of Pragmatism: A Symposium on H. S. Thayer's Meaning and Action: A Critical History of Pragmatism," *Transactions of the Charles S. Peirce Society: A Quarterly Journal in American Philosophy* 11 (1975).

Hartshorne, Charles. "Charles Peirce's 'One Contribution to Philosophy' and His Most Serious Mistake," in *Studies in the Philosophy of Charles Sanders Peirce,* 2d ser., ed. Edward Moore and Richard Robin. Amherst: University of Massachusetts Press, 1964.

Hausman, Carl. *Charles S. Peirce's Evolutionary Philosophy.* New York: Cambridge University Press, 1993.

———. "Eros and Agape in Creative Evolution: A Peircean Insight." *Process Studies* 4, no. 1 (1974).

———. "In and Out of Percepts." *Transactions of the Charles S. Peirce Society: A Quarterly Journal in American Philosophy* 26 (1990).

———. "Metaphorical Reference and Peirce's Dynamical Object, *Transactions of the Charles S. Peirce Society: A Quarterly Journal in American Philosophy* 23 (1987).

Helm, Bertrand. *Time and Reality in American Philosophy.* Amherst: University of Massachusetts Press, 1985.

Hintikka, Jaakko. "C. S. Peirce's 'First Real Discovery' and Its Contemporary Relevance." *The Monist* 63 (1980).

Holmes, Larry. "Peirce's Philosophy of Mind," in *Studies in the Philosophy of Charles Sanders Peirce,* 2d ser., ed. Edward Moore and Richard Robin. Amherst: University of Massachusetts Press, 1964.

Hookway, Christopher. *Peirce.* London: Routledge and Kegan Paul, 1985.

James, William. *A Pluralistic Universe. The Works of William James,* ed. Frederick Burkhardt. Cambridge: Harvard University Press, 1977.

Joswick, Hugh. "Peirce's Mathematical Model of Interpretation." *Transactions of the Charles S. Peirce Society: A Quarterly Journal in American Philosophy* 24 (1988).

Ketner, Kenneth L. "How Hintikka Misunderstood Peirce's Account of Theorematic Reasoning." *Transactions of the Charles S. Peirce Society: A Quarterly Journal in American Philosophy* 21 (1985).

Krauser, Peter. "The Three Fundamental Structural Categories of Charles S. Peirce." *Transactions of the Charles S. Peirce Society: A Quarterly Journal in American Philosophy* 13 (1977).

Kuhn, Thomas. *The Structure of Scientific Revolutions.* 2d ed. Chicago: University of Chicago Press, 1970.

Kuklick, Bruce. *The Rise of American Philosophy.* New Haven: Yale University Press, 1977.

Lachs, John. "Peirce, Santayana, and the Large Facts." *Transactions of the Charles S. Peirce Society: A Quarterly Journal in American Philosophy* 16 (1980).

Lewis, C. I. *Mind and the World Order.* New York: Dover, 1929.

Liszak, James Jakob. "Peirce's Interpretant." *Transactions of the Charles S. Peirce Society: A Quarterly Journal in American Philosophy* 26 (1990).

Lowe, Victor. "Peirce and Whitehead as Metaphysicians," in *Studies in the Philosophy of Charles Sanders Peirce,* 2d ser., ed. Edward Moore and Richard Robin. Amherst: University of Massachusetts Press, 1964.

Madden, Edward. "Chance and Counterfacts in Wright and Peirce." *Review of Metaphysics* 9 (1955–56).

_____. "Discussing James and Peirce With Meyers." *Transactions of the Charles S. Peirce Society: A Quarterly Journal in American Philosophy* 25 (1989).

McCarthy, Jeremiah. "Peirce's Proof of Pragmatism." *Transactions of the Charles S. Peirce Society: A Quarterly Journal in American Philosophy* 26 (1990).

McDermott, John J. *Streams of Experience: Reflections on the History and Philosophy of American Culture.* Amherst: University of Massachusetts Press, 1986.

Michael, Fred. "The Deduction of Categories in Peirce's 'New List.'" *Transactions of the Charles S. Peirce Society: A Quarterly Journal in American Philosophy* 16 (1980).

_____. "Two Forms of Scholastic Realism in Peirce's Philosophy." *Transactions of the Charles S. Peirce Society: A Quarterly Journal in American Philosophy* 24 (1988).

Murphey, Murray. *The Development of Peirce's Philosophy* Cambridge: Harvard University Press, 1961.

_____. "On Pierce's Metaphysics." *Transactions of the Charles S. Peirce Society: A Quarterly Journal in American Philosophy* 1, no. 1 (1965).

Noble, N. A. Brian. "Peirce's Definitions of Continuity and the Concept of Possibility." *Transactions of the Charles S. Peirce Society: A Quarterly Journal in American Philosophy* 25 (1989).

Oehler, Klaus. "Is a Transcendental Foundation of Semiotics Possible? A Peircean Consideration." *Transactions of the Charles S. Peirce Society: A Quarterly Journal in American Philosophy* 23 (1987).

Olshewsky, Thomas. "A Third Dogma of Empiricism." *The Monist* 49 (1965).

Pape, Helmut. "Laws of Nature, Rules of Conduct and their Analogy in Peirce's Semiotics." *Transactions of the Charles S. Peirce Society: A Quarterly Journal in American Philosophy* 20 (1984).

Potter, Vincent. *Charles S. Peirce on Norms and Ideals.* Amherst: University of Massachusetts Press, 1967.

Rescher, Nicholas. *Peirce's Philosophy of Science.* Notre Dame: University of Notre Dame Press, 1978.

Rosensohn, William L. *The Phenomenology of Charles S. Peirce*. Amsterdam: B. R. Gruner, 1974.

Roth, Robert. "Did Peirce Answer Hume on Necessary Connection?" *The Review of Metaphysics* 38 (1985).

Savan, David. "Decision and Knowledge in Peirce." *Transactions of the Charles S. Peirce Society: A Quarterly Journal in American Philosophy* 1 (1965).

———. "On the Origins of Peirce's Phenomenology," in *Studies in the Philosophy of Charles Sanders Peirce,* ed. Philip Wiener and Frederic Young. Cambridge: Harvard University Press, 1952.

———. "Response to T. L. Short." *Transactions of the Charles S. Peirce Society: A Quarterly Journal in American Philosophy* 22 (1986).

Scheffler, Israel. *Four Pragmatists: A Critical Introduction to Peirce, James, Mead and Dewey.* New York: Humanities Press, 1974.

Short, T. L. "David Savan's Peirce Studies." *Transactions of the Charles S. Peirce Society: A Quarterly Journal in American Philosophy* 22 (1986).

———. "Life among the Legisigns." *Transactions of the Charles S. Peirce Society: A Quarterly Journal in American Philosophy* 18 (1982).

———. "Peirce and the Incommensurability of Theories," in *The Relevance of Charles Peirce,* ed. Eugene Freeman. The Monist Library of Philosophy. La Salle, Ill.: Hegeler Institute, 1983.

———. "Semeiosis and Intentionality." *Transactions of the Charles S. Peirce Society: A Quarterly Journal in American Philosophy* 17 (1981).

———. "What They Said in Amsterdam: Peirce's Semiotic Today." *Semiotica* 60 (1986).

Skagestad, Peter. "Pragmatic Realism: The Peircean Argument Reexamined." *The Review of Metaphysics* 33 (1980).

———. *The Road of Inquiry: Charles Peirce's Pragmatic Realism.* New York: Columbia University Press, 1981.

Smith, John E. *Purpose and Thought: The Meaning of Pragmatism.* New Haven: Yale University Press.

Smyth, Richard. "Peirce's Examination of Mill's Philosophy," *Transactions of the Charles S. Peirce Society: A Quarterly Journal in American Philosophy* 21 (1985).

Stearn, Isabel. "Firstness, Secondness, and Thirdness," in *Studies in the Philosophy of Charles Sanders Peirce,* ed. Philip Wiener and Frederic Young. Cambridge: Harvard University Press, 1952.

Thayer, H. S. *Meaning and Action: A Critical History of Pragmatism.* Indianapolis and New York: Bobbs-Merrill Co., 1968.

———. "Reply to Criticisms." *Transactions of the Charles S. Peirce Society: A Quarterly Journal in American Philosophy* 11 (1975).

Thompson, Manley. "Peirce's Experimental Proof of Scholastic Realism," in *Studies in the Philosophy of Charles Sanders Peirce,* 2d ser., ed.

Edward Moore and Richard Robin. Amherst: University of Massachusetts Press, 1964.

———. "Pierce's Verificationist Realism." *The Review of Metaphysics* 23 (1978).

Tiles, J. E. "Iconic Thought and the Scientific Imagination." *Transactions of the Charles S. Peirce Society: A Quarterly Journal in American Philosophy* 24 (1988).

Turley, Peter. *Peirce's Cosmology.* New York: Philosophical Library, 1977.

Wennerberg, Hjalmar. *The Pragmatism of C. S. Peirce.* Lund: CWK Gleerup; Copenhagen: Ejnar Munksgaard, 1962.

Whitehead, A. N. *Process and Reality.* New York: Harper and Brothers, 1957.

Wiener, Philip. "Peirce's Evolutionary Interpretations of the History of Science," in *Studies in the Philosophy of Charles Sanders Peirce,* ed. Philip Wiener and Frederic Young. Cambridge: Harvard University Press, 1952.

INDEX